The Numerology Handbook

*The complete numerological guide
to successful everyday living*

P A U L   R O D R I G O

quantum
LONDON • NEW YORK • TORONTO • SYDNEY

quantum

The Publishing House, Bennetts Close,
Cippenham, Berkshire SL1 5AP, England.

ISBN 0-572-02214-X
Copyright © 1996 W Foulsham & Co Ltd.

Cover photograph: *Newton* by William Blake (1757–1827), Tate Gallery, London / Bridgeman Art Library, London.

Typeset by Poole Typesetting (Wessex) Ltd.
Printed in Great Britain by St. Edmundsbury Press Ltd, Bury St. Edmunds, Suffolk

CONTENTS

Events will take their course, it is no good
Our being angry at them; he is happiest
Who wisely turns them to best account.

Euripides Bellerophon. Frag. 298.

THE POWER OF NUMBERS

NUMBERS ARE EVERYWHERE

If He exists at all, God is a mathematician. This is because everything, literally everything, in creation is ordered by number. The movement of the Earth, the Sun, the Moon, all the planets and all the stars as they race across the heavens is pre-determined; their courses are plottable to the *n*th degree by mathematics. The atom, the basic unit of matter in the universe, is a mathematically arranged structure of neutrons, protons and electrons. The building block of life itself, DNA in molecular form, is constructed according to strict mathematical principles, and the code formed by the DNA molecules on the chromosome chain is a numerical arrangement which determines the transmission of genes from generation to generation. So the universe and all that it contains, even life, is a vast mathematical structure, a fantastically complicated pattern of numbers, and its complexity in no way detracts from this simple fact.

The ancient science of numerology does not pretend to unravel this extraordinary complexity. But by observation and experiment over the centuries, numerologists have discovered that numbers can be used to help understand the mysteries of the human soul (psyche), and so to analyse human personality with a reasonable degree of accuracy. Also, by skilled interpretation numerology makes it possible to predict future events. At the very least it can teach you to control your life more effectively through interaction with the workings of fate.

Numerology by its very nature is mysterious. Some people fight shy of it because it is outside their usual understanding. It can be seen as a body of mystic learning not readily accessible to their intelligence at the level of its basic functioning, and can seem remote from the down-to earth, practical approach to living they need to get through each day. If they give it a chance, they may still be suspicious because the power of numbers might seem to threaten to take from them the ultimate responsibility for their own lives. In fact it does no such thing – it enables people to put their lives into proper perspective. They are then able to build on the heightened awareness which results, to work towards a happier and more fulfilled existence.

ORIGIN OF NUMEROLOGY

Modern numerology had its beginnings in the teachings of the Greek mathematician, philosopher and mystic, Pythagoras. He lived in the sixth century BC and founded a school of philosophy at Croton, the beautiful Greek city in southern Italy. Pythagoras's contribution to the history of thought is great indeed. Every schoolchild learns the theorem for a right-angled triangle which bears his name. But his ideas went far beyond geometry. He believed that the soul is immortal – a revolutionary idea in its time – and that it passes in succession through many bodies (metempsychosis). Although he did not specifically reject the gods of mythology, he was the first Greek to represent God as a single deity, believing that likeness to the deity was the most worthy and noble aim of man in his daily work. This was an idea of morality never advanced in Greece before and anticipated the ethical ideas of both Christianity and Islam which related 'the good life' of believers on Earth to the goodness of God.

Pythagoras also built a complete metaphysical system around his grand concept of the Music of the Spheres. According to these ideas, everything in the universe forms a harmonious whole consisting of one great musical chorus. The Earth is a sphere, not flat as was generally believed then. It revolves around the central fire of the Sun and makes music as it does so. Similarly the motions of the planets produce musical sounds. Although human beings are unable to hear the Music of the Spheres, the whole of the natural world, the lives of men and women included, functions as part of this single harmony.

Realising that music is nothing more than a series of vibrations, Pythagoras was the first to discover the numerical ratios of intervals in the musical scale. Thus he bridged the gap between the universal musical chorus and number, contending that 'numbers are the principle of all things'.

According to Pythagoras, each number has a personality of its own and vibrates just like the notes in the musical scale. Some numbers have a stronger vibration than others. Odd numbers are more powerful and they are therefore regarded as masculine, whereas even numbers, less strong, are feminine. Odd numbers dominate because when odd is added to even, an odd number is always the result.

Also, the human soul or pysche, which is central to human personality, is fixed at birth and can be divided into the nine character stereotypes of the nine primary numbers, 1 to 9. It is here that the numerology of today joins forces with the ideas of Pythagoras, and this is the significance of birth numbers which is discussed in extensive detail in Chapter 2.

MODERN NUMEROLOGY

The idea of vibration, described by number, is central to numerology. Everything in the world is vibrating. Your personality is decided by the particular vibration in force at birth. Your thoughts are the vibrations which initiate and power action. So as far as events in your life are concerned, when the vibrations of personality interact with the vibrations of time, they produce specific situations and possible reactions to them. In addition, one numerical vibration may be in harmony with that of another number, in opposition to others or merely passive to them. All these interactions form the basis for the numerological life-guide presented in Chapter 3. No-one knows why predictions based on combinations of numbers work, only that they do. Because they work, you can gain insight into human psychology and your reactions to events which you cannot otherwise readily obtain.

WHY USE NUMEROLOGY?

Of course, a sceptic would argue that it is ridiculous to believe in something that cannot be explained by logic or natural science. But is it really so ridiculous? The great explorers of history had only stars and a compass to steer them into the unknown. They did not understand why the compass did the job they required of it but were sure that it was a reliable instrument for their purposes. That was enough to make possible the discovery of the New World – far beyond the shores of Europe.

Again, a rationalist would ask 'How, just by converting the numbers of the day, month and year of a person's birth to a single number from 1 to 9, can the key to personality be revealed?' and 'How can that person's fate in later life be charted by further calculations based on the movement of time?' The answer is that such calculations are no more irrational than the fact that for centuries sages have plotted the motion of the planets and stars to unravel the destiny of men and women, or that even today Chinese philosophers, and indeed ordinary Chinese citizens, throw yarrow stalks to determine what section of the Confucian oracular book, the *I Ching*, to consult in order to discover the solution to their problems. As astrology was good enough for Nostradamus – whose prophecies have continually astonished the world since medieval times – and as the *I Ching* has guided Chinese statesmen and thinkers of the Confucian school throughout ancient and modern Chinese history, then why shouldn't the mystic science of numerology, originated by Pythagoras in ancient Greece, provide vital clues about how people with a particular kind of personality can best deal with their fate at each step in life to achieve for themselves a happier and more successful existence?

If you count yourself among the doubters, then using numerology with an open mind is most likely to persuade you. Try it and see. If it works for you, well and good. If not, forget it and find something else. Once non-believers are confronted by its insights, they will find that numerology has a lot more to offer than they expected.

NUMEROLOGY IN HISTORY

Apart from the science founded by Pythagoras, numerological procedures of one sort or another have been used over the ages. The Hebrew Kabbalists sought enlightenment from sacred texts by converting words and letters to numbers. These techniques were religious in inspiration, but numerology has also gained much credibility in the secular tradition of Western thought.

For example Count Leo Tolstoy, the great Russian novelist and one of the most influential thinkers of his time, was entirely convinced of the power of numerology. Born on 8 August (old style calendar) in 1828, Tolstoy came to regard 28 as a number of vital importance in his destiny, and this was confirmed for him subsequently when his son and heir, Sergei was also born on the 28th day of a month.

For the rest of his days Tolstoy was always at great pains to give the utmost prominence to the number 28 in his writings as well as in his life. When selecting French modernist poetry in support of his treatise 'What is Art?', he chose poems from page 28 of various poetry books. Although he stated that this was to rid his work of bias, the force of 28 as a power in his life must have been uppermost in his mind. In his novel *Resurrection*, he made its hero, Prince Nekhlyudov, undergo his spiritual renaissance on 28 April. And in his greatest artistic achievement, *War and Peace*, Tolstoy also included numerology in the epic narrative of the rise and fall of Napoleon Bonaparte. Pierre Bezukhov, the would-be assassin of Napoleon, links the Apocalyptic 'number of the beast', 666 (*The Revelation* of St John the Divine, Chapter 13, Verse 18) to the arch-fiend's name by converting the letters in *'l'empereur Napoleon'* to numbers from the French alphabet enumerated in the manner of the Hebrew Kabbalistic system.

Tolstoy remained convinced of the mystic force of 28 in his own life to the very end, choosing 28 October, just before his death, to leave his beloved home at Yasnaya Polyana.

For Tolstoy, the number 28 was a fadic number, that is a number of fate (see Chapter 4) rather than a birth number for life. The Kabbalistic method of converting letter to number is the origin of a modern branch of numerology which, using similar conversions, concentrates on names as the fundamental basis of character analysis by number. This book, however, uses the system of date conversion which is now generally recognised as most reliable and accurate.

BIRTH NUMBER

The system of date conversion can be used to find out your birth number for life. This is done by taking your birth date and reducing it to a number between 1 and 9. The birth number can then be used to analyse personality and guide your actions. Chapter 2 shows you how to find out a person's birth number and describes all the personality types.

THE POWER OF NUMBER

In many facets of life, the power of numbers is very strong. This book offers a modern reinterpretation of an ancient science based on that power. If it does not actually change your life, then at the very least it will show you how to move more securely and with a greater sense of purpose along the path you have already chosen to follow towards short term and long term fulfilment.

BIRTH NUMBERS

INTRODUCTION

It is simple to work out a person's birth number. First, find out the day, month and year in which they were born. Next, write out their date of birth in numerical form. So for someone born on 12 October 1966, set down the numbers like this:

Stage 1:	**12 / 10 / 1966**

Then add together the numbers in the three component parts, keeping them separate at this stage:

Stage 2:	**1 + 2 = 3; 1 + 0 = 1; 1 + 9 + 6 + 6 = 22**

Now add the three totals together:

Stage 3:	**3 + 1 + 22 = 26**

Since we are concerned only with the primary numbers 1 to 9, the final stage is to add the numbers together until you get 9 or less:

Stage 4:	**2 + 6 = 8**

So this person has a birth number of 8.

Here are two more examples to get the procedure absolutely clear in your mind:

	15 July 1941
Stage 1:	**15 / 7 / 1941**
Stage 2:	**1 + 5 = 6; 7; 1 + 9 + 4 + 1 = 15**
Stage 3:	**6 + 7 + 15 = 28**
Stage 4:	**2 + 8 = 10 and 1 + 0 = 1**
Birth number:	**1**

Note that in the last example on the next page, before the final reduction to 4, the birth date makes 22. This, like 11, is a master number in numerology and its significance is explained at the end of this chapter. So that you can check for the numbers 11 or 22 in character analysis, you

	12 November 1916
Stage 1:	**12 / 11 / 1916**
Stage 2:	**1 + 2 = 3; 1 + 1 = 2; 1 + 9 + 1 + 6 = 17**
Stage 3:	**3 + 2 + 17 = 22**
Stage 4:	**2 + 2 = 4**
Birth number:	**4**

must reduce the birth date numbers exactly as shown above. If you use a short cut, such as 12 + 11 + 1 + 9 + 1 + 6 = 40 and 4 + 0 = 4, you would still get a birth number of 4, but you would miss the special number 22, and this could have a great effect on the accuracy of the character reading.

Use this page to work out your birth number and those of people significant to you.

Name	_____
Birth date	___/___/_____
Stage 1:	_____
Stage 2:	_____
Stage 3:	_____
Stage 4:	_____
Birth Number:	_____

Name	_____
Birth date	___/___/_____
Stage 1:	_____
Stage 2:	_____
Stage 3:	_____
Stage 4:	_____
Birth Number:	_____

Name	_____
Birth date	___/___/_____
Stage 1:	_____
Stage 2:	_____
Stage 3:	_____
Stage 4:	_____
Birth Number:	_____

So when you begin to analyse personality according to the birth number profiles in this chapter, remember to look for numbers 11 or 22 at stage 3 when you are finding the birth number. Then you can use the analysis of the birth number you found and, if you also found numbers 11 or 22 at stage 3, you should check that analysis too.

PERSONALITY TYPES

So, apart from numbers 11 and 22, numerology allows for nine basic human types. Individuals of a particular number will come from many different walks of life, and very few people will exactly match the character profile indicated by their birth number. But everyone born with a given number will have many elements of that number's stereotype in their personality. They will all be dealt roughly the same cards at birth, some good, some bad. How they play these cards, making the most of the better ones and overcoming the weaknesses possible from the indifferent ones, will determine the level of fulfilment they achieve in life.

Very occasionally there are people who do not seem to correspond in any way to the profile indicated by their birth number. They are not the exceptions that prove the rule. Rather they are persons who are completely out of touch with the psychic core of their being. Close study of this book, and of the advice it offers, can help such unfortunate individuals get back to the true path they were meant to follow.

For the vast majority, the numbered personality profile will be a very fair summary of many of their major character traits. But this book is not written just for interest. It is intended to help you and the best way it can do this is to help you help yourself.

The first stage in this process is self-awareness, as this brings self-control and the ability to fit personality to circumstances for the best possible outcome of a situation. Surprisingly perhaps, very few people really know themselves and in some cases might be horrified if they could see themselves as others see them. Most people have a reasonable idea of their good points, but tend to overlook or are even unaware of the bad ones. Even if they admit to a fault, they prefer to minimise its importance, telling themselves that the bad is far outweighed by the good. Very few make any real attempt to eliminate or improve on traits they know in their hearts to be failings of character. What they do do is forgive themselves for these failings. Because nearly everybody is vain and self-centred, they think the rest of the world will forgive them too. 'You will just have to take me as you find me,' is an excuse you often hear. But such people don't realise that their failings are not only to a greater or lesser extent unacceptable to others, they are actually harmful to their own well-being.

Of course few people are all bad. Most of us have attractive features to our personalities and possess some talents or abilities. But we do not always know exactly what we are best at, or what is the full extent of our capabilities. This can often result in a sense of frustration, even failure. Numerology, as it is presented in the following pages, offers you a golden opportunity for a journey of self-discovery which will enable you to make the most of your natural advantages and also to channel your weaknesses in more positive directions.

People born under the Number 1 vibration, for example, are on the whole insensitive to other people's feelings and bad at relationships. But leaders often need to stand alone without paying too much attention to the affection of the crowd. They are the ones to make unpopular decisions from which they and others can profit, even if they gain only respect but little real love from their subordinates.

People born under Number 2, on the other hand, are mainly secretive souls, yet in some areas of life discretion is a valuable asset, highly prized because our capacity for it is so limited.

Are you stubborn? Number 8 people certainly are, but someone somewhere may need that grit and determination and could come to depend on it.

Perfectionists can get a bit of a bore at times, but close attention to detail and a talent for precise analysis are vital in many jobs and undertakings. This is exactly where the dull, plodding Number 4 person excels!

So in this book you will find out exactly who you are, what really makes you tick and how you come across to others. You can then learn how to make more of your strengths and divert your weaknesses into productive channels. This can lead to a more contented life.

COLOUR

Colour has an important part to play in numerology as it affects your life. Most people underestimate the importance of colour in everyday living. It can greatly enhance your personality and can strongly influence how others react to you. It is a very subtle form of body language and though simple to use, can materially affect your progress in life.

Every numerical vibration is linked to a particular colour or combination of shades. These colour affinities are described in this book. By using them in your dress, or even in something so apparently inconsequential as the colour of your car or the interior decor of your house, you can make the best of yourself. Through colour you can bring out the most powerful and attractive aspects of your personality, and so maximise your potential. At ease with yourself, you can influence other people in ways that advance your interests when they respond to colours which emphasise your good points.

NUMBER 1

The inner conflict – opposing facets of the Number 1 personality

POSITIVE	NEGATIVE
Showman	Introvert
Self-confident	Egocentric
Emotional	Petty
Independent	Uncaring
Single-minded	Self-centred
Natural ability	Overconfidence
Brainy	Opinionated
Special talents	Obsessions
High standards	Narrow vision
Skilled in organisation	Bad at relationships
Great expectations	Frustrated ambitions
Likely to succeed	No stomach for a fight
Leader	Tyrant
Outwardly successful	Inwardly disappointed
Rise	Fall
Craves affection	Covets material rewards
Passionate	Lonely
Sexually alluring	Unsensual
Conventional home life	Domestic strife
Paternal or maternal	Domineering
Fulfilled	Bitter

PERSONALITY

For the Greeks, Number 1, being the first in the transcendent sequence of primary numbers, was above all the number of potential. So Number 1 signifies the most creative and progressive elements in human capacity, even if all those who live under its influence are not necessarily able, for one reason or another, to take full advantage of the favourable signs of their birth.

Number 1 mostly rules the mind. So Number 1 people are nearly always intelligent and may instinctively prefer abstract thought to its practical applications. At the same time they are usually ambitious and make natural leaders in all walks of life. Without being obviously flamboyant, they often have the personal magnetism of the showman who can carry others with them by sheer force of personality. They are likely to aim for the top, and often get there. If they do succeed, they may well succeed magnificently. Just look at the list at the end of this chapter of famous people of this number, living or dead, and note how many of them are or were the undisputed 'No. 1' in their field.

That is the positive side of Number 1, but the negative aspects of the number mean that not every person with this vibration will automatically be a success in life. Whatever their natural gifts, Number 1s are not always brimming with the self-confidence necessary to exploit them – just the reverse in some cases. Many need to learn assertiveness in order to overcome their fear of taking the lead. The cut and thrust of life can teach them valuable lessons about the importance of pushing themselves skilfully to the forefront. If they remain on the side-lines, it may be because they are weak and indecisive, or even careless and lazy.

Either way they are almost always self-centred. They tend to see everything and everybody only in terms of themselves, and will sulk if they do not get their own way. If they are confronted with problems or difficulties which they are unable to cope with, their misplaced vanity does not always allow them to seek the help of others when this would be the wisest course to follow. Their tendency to be overbearing may have unfortunate consequences both for their progress in life and for their relations with other people. Should everything not run as smoothly as they hope and expect, their conceit degenerates all too easily into bossiness and a petulant disregard for others – whom they look on as their inferiors, often in spite of all the evidence. If this tendency is not controlled, they can become disappointed and bitter when their standing in the world turns out to be different to their own high opinion of their true worth.

Even for those of this number who do find worldly success, their self-centred approach to life has many pitfalls. They like praise. This is true for us all, but Number 1s go out of their way to encourage it from those around them. Whether it is deserved or not, they need praise to boost the self-esteem which spurs them on to higher things. However, there is a fine line between praise and flattery, and by choosing admir-ers rather than true friends they limit their chances of having satisfac-tory relationships. In extreme cases this can threaten the completion of their material aims. Not all tyrants are born with Number 1 as their life number, but nearly all Number 1s have the seeds of tyranny hidden within their psyche. Single-mindedness can be very expensive in human terms and a lot of Number 1 people are prepared, consciously or uncon-sciously, to sacrifice respect, friendship, even love to get what they want. They have very strong feelings and opinions. The unshakeable inner conviction that they must be right can cause them to brush aside other people in a careless and uncaring manner. Often solitary by tempera-ment, this makes a lot of them very lonely indeed as they gather the trappings of material success around them to reassure themselves of their own value as human beings.

Number 1 people are frequently attracted to the professions, where intellectual ability is at a premium, but they are seldom content to be just 'one of the crowd' even when they find work they like. The typical Number 1 solicitor secretly longs to be a barrister or a judge; the Number 1 family doctor asks himself with a sigh why he spends his days writing out routine prescriptions instead of doing the glamorous job of a hospi-tal consultant. Actors and actresses always have one eye on the very top of the bill. Academic gifts lead many Number 1s into teaching, but lack of opportunity to use their organisational powers can frustrate them.

The role of head teacher seems much more interesting than that of a form master or mistress. The science teacher with his bunsen burner and GCSE syllabus dreams of doing research that will lead to a great discovery and lasting fame. Number 1s do well as journalists and writers, but the urge to be in control makes them want to be editors or departmental chiefs, not just staff reporters or mere contributors.

Number 1 is an austere number and brings a serious frame of mind so it can lead some Number 1 people into the religious life. Even here they cannot help their own natures. The humble minister really believes he could do the bishop's work better than the bishop himself.

If you are a Number 1 and you recognise yourself in any of these sketches, you should remember that not everyone can reach the top. And anyway, the path to the top is not always a royal road to true contentment. But the highly developed ambitious streak of so many Number 1s means that they succeed at high levels while many others of a different vibration fall short, regardless of their inherent, potential abilities.

Not every Number 1 is an 'intellectual'. As children they can be quite ordinary at school, but they are nearly always creative or gifted in some way. This could be in some branch of the arts, or they may excel at sports in general or at one sport in particular – where they seem to possess an innate talent which distinguishes them. In business life they can have a ready grasp of what is required to bring success – a mixture of down-to-earth common sense and native cunning which cuts through to essentials and gets the job done.

Nor is every Number 1 ambitious in the ordinary sense. Some, particularly men, of this vibration have a fierce independence which can lead them to pursue life goals they value greatly, but which are much less highly regarded by society as a whole. So they may dedicate themselves to a personal obsession which does not necessarily bring the material rewards of conventional success.

Not all Number 1 women will be career women, though many of them are. Some prefer marriage and a family, but then are likely to transfer their ambitious instincts to their husbands and offspring, pushing them on in their careers and doing everything they can to ensure their children's success at school and beyond. As a wife, the typical Number 1 woman is seldom passive as a partner. She is often tough and demanding, and may try to dominate every aspect of home life. If she does not hold the whip hand in both big and small things, she may scheme ruthlessly to attain her ends or engineer a row for no other purpose than to get the upper hand, using her femininity in an aggressive way to dominate. Once her power is secure, she will be absolutely loyal to her man, even secretly doting on him, though as a matter of policy she is not likely to let it show either to others or to her husband himself.

Number 1 people who don't have its more serious character defects do not know their own strength. It is second nature for them to push as hard as they can in what they see as their own best interests – but sometimes they are a bit too forceful and insensitive in the way they do it. This can create enemies or begin to alienate loved ones or friends who lack their mental toughness, or who can't turn a blind eye to the extremes of the Number 1's inner drives.

Yet in general, Number 1 is a favourable birth number. Those born under its influence are mostly independent, creative people with good powers of concentration and more often than not, a dignified bearing which commands respect from others. Many of them enjoy life to the full, but because they tend to set the highest standards for themselves, frustration is never far away as a potential threat to complete fulfilment. This can affect their approach to career, love, marriage, children and friendship, and may even extend to hobbies and leisure pursuits as well as the trifling details of daily life.

As reflective people who basically prefer their own company, they often show a surprising ability to move easily among all kinds of people in the manner of the true extrovert – but nearly always with an element of calculation or self-seeking. In unfavourable circumstances, they can fall prey to the kind of fears that often accompany extreme introversion. When they meet major difficulties or setbacks, they do not always respond well, as they may sometimes lack the resilience of the true fighter.

Finding themselves 'banging their head against a brick wall', real or imagined, their energy may turn in negative directions to the detriment of themselves and those around them. Number 1s who are outwardly successful can have deep, inner frustration – a pyschological quirk arising from limited vision that demands perfection in everything. In an extreme form this can cause harm in all sorts of ways both expected and unexpected, and once again the chief sufferer will probably be themselves. If Number 1s are most likely to be life's achievers, it is also true that a lot of trouble in the world is caused by people of this number who are frustrated in some way.

In matters of love and sex, Number 1 people may have many relationships in their early adult years and they often experience difficulty in settling down with one partner. They lean towards members of the other sex who share their serious outlook on life – but in such meetings of minds, passion which is also important to them, may be lacking. They are very status-conscious in their attitude to courtship and marriage; the prince goes in search of his princess and *vice versa*. It is not easy to find both brains and beauty, so it can be a long time before the typical Number 1 finds the sexual and intellectual chemistry to match their ideal.

Most Number 1s are sexually vigorous and they can bring highly charged emotion to a sexual situation in a way that is irresistible. But they may not be especially sensual. They can have an unfortunate tendency to view love-making as a means of expressing and imposing dominance. Anyone involved with a Number 1 lover should be aware of this and be prepared to accommodate it before making a final commitment. Many Number 1s of both sexes fail to realise that, for marriage or a permanent relationship to have the best chance of lasting success it should be a partnership of equals in and out of the bedroom. This can cause serious emotional problems for both parties.

But Number 1 is the father of numbers according to Pythagoras, and men and women with this vibration generally make loving parents. Family in the dynastic sense is very important to them, so the birth of a child is an event to be celebrated not just because of the spontaneous joy it brings but because it carries forward the family from one generation to the next. A Number 1 person, therefore, is likely to be a very committed parent. Number 1s and their offspring usually form a very close bond which grows as the years pass and which is likely to endure through thick and thin.

Because they want to rule the roost in so much of their lives, Number 1s should take care not to dominate a child, even through love. Always 'knowing best', always controlling rather than guiding – this can smother developing infants who will need to become independent to take their own place in the world outside the protected atmosphere of the home.

Everyone needs a comfortable, contented domestic life and in this respect Number 1s, with or without children, are no exception. Their ambitions can expose them to pressures which could tempt them to neglect their home for their career. They should have the good sense to realise that a haven from the cares of the 'rat race' is the best guarantee of peace and stability in their lives.

There certainly should be no domestic strain due to lack of money, though many Number 1s have a taste for the 'best of everything' which may get out of hand if they don't restrain themselves. But on the whole nearly all Number 1s are 'good providers'. Number 1 women, if they have not continued their career while their children were growing up, are very likely to go back to work as soon as they can. For the most talented Number 1s, earnings from a second or unusual source can often add to the main family income. If on the other hand money is tight, the typical Number 1, particularly if a man, feels inadequate and this may cause disharmony which could poison what was otherwise a contented marriage.

However there is one weakness which all Number 1 people can show in financial matters. It stems from their inner certainty that their judgement is seldom, if ever, wrong. So they may overestimate their skill in investments and other complicated financial arrangements. Unless they are trained in finance, they should not let their ego stand in the way of seeking and acting upon the advice of professionals.

Number 1s work hard and play hard. They usually have a robust constitution but, even so, they should avoid overdoing it. They tend to burn the candle at both ends, and this might lead to problems sooner or later. If they become ill, it is most likely to come out of the blue. Yet with hindsight the warning signs were probably there all the time.

Their characteristic liking for strenuous sports as a way of relaxing is another symptom of their natural inclination to drive themselves hard. Outdoor games such as football or rugby, or indoor ones like squash and badminton seem to attract them as a release from their more intellectual preoccupations. There is little potential harm in this if their overall health is sound.

Life in general seems to have a way of sneaking up on Number 1s when they least expect it. The more successful they become, the truer this can be. A lot of Number 1s rise meteorically in the world, only to be plunged from the heights by an unkind fate and inherent weaknesses they have failed to correct. Even the moderately successful among them are always hankering after that little bit of extra success which may put at risk their existing achievements. For those who do not attain their most cherished life goals, their sense of relative failure comes from the excess pride and egocentricity which afflicts all Number 1s to some degree.

People of this vibration, though born with many advantages, must find a balance between the contrary impulses which both push them forward and hold them back. Except for the weaker ones who have to gain strength from time and experience, order and stability are not a problem for them, because they are basically self-reliant and tenacious with a disciplined approach to living. But they are prone to excesses in thought, word and deed that sometimes bring serious disruption, even disaster, in their wake. How Number 1 people deal with this fundamental contradiction of character will determine not only the course of their lives, but also their ultimate happiness.

NUMBER 1 CHILDREN

Great care may be needed from parents of Number 1 children to ensure that they have the best chance of developing into balanced personalities. When very young, Number 1 children are likely to be independent, lonely youngsters, frequently withdrawn and uncommunicative among people their own age. Often they prefer the company of adults. This could produce an unhealthy precocity – so they need to be encouraged to mix freely with other children. Failure to join in enough may mean they go into adolescence as isolated outsiders, and this could create many serious problems when they have to make their own way in the adult world.

Once the ice is broken with other children, Number 1s tend to be bossy and try to dominate their playmates. Parents need to stop conflicts which could lead to frustration and even destructive behaviour if a forceful Number 1 cannot gain the upper hand over others who will not accept a subordinate role. Children of this vibration have to learn to assert themselves in ways that do not alienate their fellows. This is the best guarantee that their qualities of leadership will emerge fully later on.

A Number 1 child who is not doing well at school should not be made to feel guilty. More than any other vibration, Number 1s find their own way, and any attempt to force them in directions they do not wish to go will probably be counter-productive. However, any tendency towards laziness or a couldn't-care-less attitude should be corrected very firmly.

COLOUR

Psychologists as well as numerologists have noted that yellow is favoured by people who are convinced of their own importance and who wish to impress others. The 'yellow personality' is invariably ambitious. So, Number 1 has always been linked with yellow; for those who feel that this is just not their colour, gold and brown have a similar affinity.

For Number 1 people, yellow, or its shades, as signal of their inner selves, will produce in others the kind of reaction to them that they want. If Number 1s are disappointed or unfulfilled in some way, they may subconsciously avoid yellow. This is an error, for yellow is a talisman for the future, and brings hope and the determination to succeed, whatever the obstacles.

FAMOUS NUMBER 1 PEOPLE

☆ **Monarch** ☆
★ Elizabeth I of England ★
  ☆ **Modern British Royalty** ☆
★ Duchess of Gloucester, Prince Harry, Duke of Kent, ★
  Duke of York
☆ **Politicians** ☆
★ Joseph Goebbels, Mikhail Gorbachev, Roy Hattersley, Keith ★
  Joseph, Ian Paisley, David Steel, Norman Tebbit, Lech Walesa
☆ **Soldier/politician** ☆
★ Napoleon Bonaparte ★
☆ **Religious Leader** ☆
★ Mother Teresa ★
☆ **Scientist** ☆
★ Fred Hoyle ★
☆ **Thinkers** ☆
★ Karl Marx, Blaise Pascal ★
☆ **Explorer** ☆
★ Jacques Cousteau ★
☆ **Entrepreneur** ☆
★ Rupert Murdoch ★
☆ **Writers** ☆
★ Emily Brontë, Noel Coward, Salman Rushdie, Percy B. Shelley, ★
  Leo Tolstoy, Colin Wilson, Virginia Woolf, Emile Zola
☆ **Musicians** ☆
★ Anton Bruckner, Bernard Haitink, Ivor Novello, Ringo Starr, ★
  Malcolm Williamson
☆ **Singers** ☆
★ José Carreras, Enrico Caruso, Maurice Chevalier, ★
  Placido Domingo
☆ **Actors and actresses** ☆
★ Ingrid Bergman, Humphrey Bogart, Sean Connery, ★
  Rita Hayworth, John Hurt, Jerry Lewis, Sophia Loren,
  Jack Nicholson, Robert Redford

☆   **Media personalities** ☆
★ Russ Abbot, Ronnie Barker, Angus Deayton, Walt Disney, Peter ★
  Hall, Rolf Harris, Des O'Connor, Willie Rushton, Ernie Wise
☆   **Infamous** ☆
★ Peter Sutcliffe (the 'Yorkshire Ripper') ★
☆   **Sportsmen and women** ☆
★ Ian Botham, Ted Dexter, Paul Gascoigne, Len Hutton, ★
  Stanley Matthews, Alain Prost

NUMBER 2

The inner conflict – opposing facets of the Number 2 personality

POSITIVE	NEGATIVE
Compassionate	Over-sensitive
Selfless	Vindictive
Good friend	Bad enemy
Carer	Limited aspirations
Warm-hearted	Mean
Outward calm	Emotional depth
Discreet	Secretive
Gifted	Ordinary
Sound judgement	Self-doubt
Able	Uncompetitive
Easy-going	Stubborn
Loves peace	Hates conflict
Natural subordinate	Reluctant leader
Lacking in ambition	Resentful of other people's success
Private compensations	Professional failures
Needs affection	Lacks passion
Loving	Possessive
Faithful	Fearful of betrayal
Domesticated	Wanderer
Careful of health	Hypochondriac

PERSONALITY

Originally identified by Pythagoras as the mother of numbers, Number 2 in women brings the compassion and passivity of the archetypal mother figure, whilst the strength of men of this number is more likely to lie in the sensitivity and tact of the truly civilised, mature human being than in the aggressive tendency of a 'macho', youthful male stereotype. But Number 2 is in opposition to Number 1, so those of both sexes born under its influence have a stubborn streak which frequently surprises anyone foolish enough to underestimate them.

Number 2s are quiet, undemonstrative people. They seldom set the world on fire and most of them have little desire to do so. Therefore they are often in a subordinate position – both in close relationships and in the workplace. This does not mean that they are incapable of taking the lead, but if they tire of the role of 'second fiddle', they have to make a deliberate and conscious effort to overcome their inclination to shy away from the limelight. That is why so many ultimately successful people of this vibration are slow starters. However, once they have got over their natural diffidence, they can be extremely tenacious in pursuit of their goals. So, by itself, Number 2 as the birth number is not necessarily a barrier to great achievement in any field of human endeavour.

Every now and then Number 2 throws up men and women who,

though perfectly ordinary in most respects, are endowed with a truly exceptional gift which brings them recognition and sometimes fame, apparently without much effort. Most Number 2 people, however, lack the competitive edge to rise to the very top. They are shrewd and cautious, and capable of imaginative thought. But too often they are not forceful enough in putting their ideas forward, nor sufficiently ruthless in advancing their own interest. They prefer peace and harmony and, with few exceptions, are rarely happy in the midst of strife. So a lot of them do best in safe occupations and are content with a routine where their ability to knuckle down makes it possible for them to create for themselves a neat, well-ordered environment where they are sheltered from turmoil and conflict.

Frequently they are ruled more by the heart than the head and, as a result, are often found in 'caring' jobs. Good-natured, tolerant and kind, they make excellent doctors, dentists, nurses and social workers. Power for its own sake seldom interests them and, should they acquire it, they are likely to see it only as a means to an end. So if they covet it at all this is only because it enables them to do something about causes which are important to them. The desire to leave the world a better place than they found it is a typical driving force of the most energetic Number 2 people. Also, their sensitivity and concern for others sometimes expresses itself in the form of a gift for clairvoyance or mediumship.

Selfless or not, however, not every Number 2 person will become one of life's winners. Most of them are loyal and discreet and think more than they say, and what they do say is usually highly valued by others. Yet, while people are ready to place great trust in their judgement, they themselves are frequently inclined to lack the courage of their convictions and their actions are not always as sensible as their opinions.

Because they are sensitive and perceptive, they can readily spot the faults of those who, unlike themselves, are prepared to ride roughshod over others to get what they want. Thwarted in their own, even limited ambitions, this can produce resentment which they will do well to suppress if they can, or at the very least hide. There is no point in making matters worse by creating powerful enemies. Nor should they give in to their tendency to get discouraged easily. If they let things get them down unduly, this will only cause worry and strain that is unnecessary and counter-productive. Life often seems unfair to them, and it often is, but they should remember that everyone has disappointments. Instead of inwardly railing against people they are in no position to challenge and against events beyond their control, they must try not to take things so much to heart and try to concentrate on the positive aspects of their lives.

Because people of this number are uncomfortable in the fight to succeed at all costs, they seek outlets in private life where they are free to pursue some personal interest or talent away from external pressures. For instance they may have above average musical, artistic or literary ability, and even if they fall short of professional standard, cultivation of their gift can be a real joy that will sustain them throughout life.

For most Number 2s their outward unflappability is their biggest asset. To paraphrase Rudyard Kipling, their ability to keep their heads when all around them are losing theirs gives them a vital inner resource denied to more volatile types. Many of the most successful people of this vibration are able to project a steely quality on the outside, even if they are seething within.

This calm, measured approach is mirrored above all in the fact that it is the peace and security of a happy home life that they value most. Many women born under Number 2 reject a serious career in favour of a happy marriage as a cushion against the harsher realities of the outside world. However Number 2 has been called the middle number, becoming good or bad by association, so female Number 2s must choose very carefully the partner to whom they entrust the sharing of their all-important domestic future. Having made their choice, they are the kind who are most likely to stick to their marriage vows for better or for worse. The breakdown of a relationship would be a bitter confession of failure which they find difficult to contemplate. So some of them cling on stubbornly in a basically unsatisfactory partnership rather than admit a defeat for which they will very probably blame themselves, whatever the true merits of the case.

For Number 2 men too, a comfortable home environment full of genuine warmth is essential for their inner contentment, far more perhaps than is the case with males of other vibrations. For them, home is not just a base to which they return each evening, but the very centre of their existence. A lot of Number 2 men, if they do not exactly 'marry their mothers', seem to prefer as life partners strong women who will build for them a secure haven that recalls the shelter and protection given by loving parents in early childhood. If this brings them the reassurance they need, it is no bad thing. However, they must accept this aspect of their nature and be prepared to come to terms with the limits this will impose on their male freedoms, or tension could arise that might threaten and perhaps destroy the fabric of domestic life, however carefully and lovingly it has been built by their partner.

But if home and hearth dominate for Number 2 people as the principal framework of reference in a happy marriage, neither the men nor the women are stick-in-the-muds. They often enjoy an active social life in which their quiet manner and unobtrusive charm make them popular with all kinds of people. They frequently have an easy sense of humour and a lightness of social touch which can endear them to both close friends and casual acquaintances.

Despite their strong preference for homely joys, they are not afraid to 'up sticks' and move on to different places in search of a better life. After all, 'home is where the heart is' and many Number 2s have a natural curiosity about the world which may take them far from their original roots. Also, a liking for living near water is an unusual trait in some of them.

With domestic life so important, the best type of partner for Number 2s of both sexes will be someone with a lot of common sense. Sexual passion may take second place to simple respect and affection, and its absence is no barrier to long-term happiness for, when the passion goes, any relationship which relies heavily upon it is not certain to endure. Although Number 2s can take physical sex or leave it, they are faithful types who expect absolute fidelity in return. As long as they feel wanted and loved on an exclusive basis everything is fine but both the men and the women easily become jealous and, if given real grounds for suspicion, can become spitefully vindictive in their single-minded determination to defend the relationship. Unfortunately, uncompromising jealousy can just as easily weaken the bonds of love as strengthen them, sometimes with the opposite effect to the one wanted.

In a successful marriage, both male and female Number 2s have a keen appreciation of domestic comfort made possible by carefully handling resources. Many of them are not the kind to attract wealth or large incomes, but money is very important to them as the cement of domestic security. So most of them are 'careful' where their finances are concerned, and some may even be mean with cash.

Psychologically they are private people. In the company of relatives or close friends they are easily stirred emotionally and sometimes readily moved to tears, but in public they are often at pains to hide their feelings under a calm exterior. If they are frustrated or unhappy, this can turn into an obsession with secrecy which could earn them an unfortunate reputation for being people with something to hide.

Along with this emotional streak, they display strong likes and dislikes, and often have the regrettable trait of never forgetting a slight, however trivial, and are liable to bear grudges. Given the opportunity they can be vengeful, secretly awaiting their chance to settle a score. They are certainly good people to have as friends, but equally anyone who treats them in what they consider an unfair or unkind way may make an implacable foe. This is an unhealthy characteristic of Number 2s, for anger and resentment are negative emotions which can hurt them just as much as their object, especially when they are unable to strike back. It is one of the very worst aspects of their personality, for animosities, bottled up for too long, may surface under pressure and, despite the customary calm of the vibration, can result in embarrassing public displays of emotion which are completely out of character and which may only lead to more trouble.

Yet the negative aspects of Number 2 need not mean a life of frustration. Number 2 people have the ability to find other outlets for their talents which may ultimately prove more satisfying than the frequently elusive, material aims of more ambitious types. However life treats them, they can always take consolation in the fact that their finest quality is their loyalty to anyone they accept as a friend or an ally. This in turn means that when things go badly, they will never lack sympathy and support.

An extension of their loyal natures is their patriotism. Number 2s are the true flag-wavers in the population. And this should be no surprise, for love of country and keeping faith with loved ones, friends and supporters are really two sides of the same coin.

The health of Number 2 people, though not always exceptionally vigorous, is usually sound enough provided care is taken. However they may be prone to minor ailments. As a response to this, they are the kind who like to reassure themselves by careful attention to diet, and are often confirmed addicts of health foods and vitamin supplements. Many are vegetarians and they are sometimes very interested in 'alternative' forms of medicine. Not exactly hypochondriacs, they are acutely aware of the importance of good health, and take a sympathetic view of any panacea which might ensure its maintenance.

Number 2s are great hoarders and collectors. As long as there are people of this vibration in the world, antique shops and collectors' fairs will never be short of customers. All their leisure pursuits are usually related in some way to the home and things which help to improve it or enhance its appearance. So they are often do-it-yourself fanatics and the women may be keen on handicrafts. Apart from the professional sports-men and women among them, they are not particularly sporty but, if they do have a sporting interest, water sports and horses are two areas which may especially attract them.

So many Number 2 people have all the virtues of the unexceptional. They like to think of themselves as 'Mr or Mrs Average', taking their standards of conduct from the consensus agreed by the majority. They believe in compromise and moderation, but can be very stubborn when they consider themselves wronged. Here they display a mixture of strength and determination that often wins the day, but in so many ways they are prepared to settle for less than the best, and find themselves tolerating weakness and injustice, thus helping to perpetuate it, for they are seldom the sort to go out on a limb whatever the cost. They may be dogmatic in their attitude to life and have strong views, but when the chips are really down, they are most likely to follow the herd or trim their sails to the wind.

Therefore the greatest problem for a typical Number 2 person is to find a role in life which reflects their own unique *persona*, yet at the same time corresponds to the conventional attitudes of which they are so much a prisoner. This is especially true for those who are not blessed with some special gift or talent that they can develop as a foun-dation for a happy and successful existence. Domestic contentment may provide a very real compensation, but if they are honest about it, they would have to admit that this is rarely enough to satisfy their deepest longings.

Here is the real paradox for so many of them. If life seems to offer great possibilities which have a way of eluding them, too often they never really know which possibilities they want to pursue. So they may lack a sense of deeply committed purpose and this can dog them all their days.

When thinking of people born under Number 2 the words of the poet Thomas Gray come readily to mind:

> Far from the madding Crowd's ignoble Strife,
> Their sober Wishes never learn'd to stray;
> Along the cool sequester'd Vale of Life
> They kept the noiseless Tenor of their Way.

However great or small their achievements in life, the fundamental decency and compassion of most Number 2 people is a certain guarantee that the world in which they lived and struggled would definitely have been a poorer place had they not been a part of it. That, as we have seen above, is often the fulfilment of their dearest wish. It is not an aspiration which anyone should make light of.

NUMBER 2 CHILDREN

Sensitive as they are, children born under this vibration are frequently labelled 'difficult' by adults who observe their early development with a knowing, but not necessarily knowledgeable eye. Superficially, Number 2 children may sometimes appear 'different' when thrown into the hurly-burly of play and competition with other youngsters, as well as in their relations with grown-ups. The truth of the matter is that the basic problem in most cases stems from the overriding need for these children to establish their own individuality.

They may not be entirely at ease with themselves or fit easily into the ready-made pattern of life established for them from birth. So, from many confused and confusing emotions which crowd in on them almost immediately, the search is on to find an identity and an image with which they themselves are comfortable and which at the same time will gain them acceptance and credibility in the world at large. The complicated blend of affection and rivalry between brothers and sisters in a large family can be a definite help, whereas an only child may be seriously disadvantaged. But for any Number 2 child, whatever their family circumstances, the quest for a coherent and unified inner and outer 'self' will never be an easy one and anything less than a complete solution to the problem may result in rebellion during adolescence and early adulthood. The consequences of a slow start in so vital an area may linger on for years, or may never be fully resolved.

Matters may be made worse by too strict an upbringing, or one in which the child is deliberately kept apart from people of his or her own age. Parents of strong moral, social or religious prejudices who rigidly impose their view of things on the developing child do them no favours at all. Supervision born of love and understanding is one thing but strict rules and regulations enforced from above are quite another for, as we have seen, Number 2 children need above all to find their feet among their peers, learning from their own experience and their own mistakes.

Children born under Number 2 often favour the parent of the opposite sex at the expense of the other. A close relationship between daughter and father or son and mother is normal enough but it can be extremely unhealthy if excessive. Any resulting resentment by the apparently rejected parent must be put to one side and the situation tactfully corrected by both parents in a caring way. Whatever outward appearances suggest, the love of both parents is essential to these children and offers the best chance of a happy and successful development.

As the years pass, particularly when they reach school age, Number 2 children will probably be faced with choices and decisions which they may find difficult to cope with. Once again guidance and support from both parents will be very important to them, provided it is not imposed in a spirit of 'we know best'. If they show early signs of some special gift or aptitude, this should be encouraged without losing sight of the need for varied interests and a balanced outlook on life.

COLOUR

Blue is the colour for Number 2s. It reflects both the calmness with which they habitually meet the travails of life and also their need for the calm, ordered environment in which they are most likely to flourish.

Psychological tests show beyond doubt that all pure shades of blue have a soothing effect on everyone within their ambience. So Number 2 people can exploit blue not only to strengthen their own inner tranquility, but to smooth their way with those they encounter in business and social life.

A preference for blue-green on the part of Number 2 persons is, however, a bad sign, indicating that the selfless aspects of their character are, temporarily at least, dormant in the face of an egocentric approach to external events in their lives.

FAMOUS NUMBER 2 PEOPLE

☆   **Monarch**   ☆
★ George V of Great Britain   ★
☆   **Modern British Royalty**   ☆
★ Princess Alexandra, Duke of Edinburgh, Anne,   ★
   the Princess Royal, Prince of Wales, Prince William
☆   **Politicians**   ☆
★ Gerry Adams, Tony Blair, Leonid Brezhnev, Leon Brittan,   ★
   Bill Clinton, Hugh Gaitskell, Al Gore, Denis Healey,
   Neil Kinnock, Helmut Kohl, Norman Lamont, Nigel Lawson,
   V. I. Lenin, Ronald Reagan, Cecil Rhodes
☆   **Soldiers/politicians**   ☆
★ Colin Powell, Duke of Wellington   ★
☆   **Philanthropist**   ☆
★ Thomas Barnardo   ★
☆   **Explorer**   ☆
★ Edmund Hillary   ★
☆   **Astronaut**   ☆
★ Yuri Gagarin   ★
☆   **Entrepreneurs**   ☆
★ Henry Ford, J. Paul Getty   ★
☆   **Writers**   ☆
★ Hans Christian Andersen, Alan Ayckbourn, Melvyn Bragg,   ★
   W. S. Gilbert, Arthur Koestler, Samuel Pepys, Beatrix Potter,
   R. L. Stevenson, Jules Verne
☆   **Artists**   ☆
★ Edouard Manet, Raphael   ★
☆   **Designer**   ☆
★ Norman Hartnell   ★
☆   **Musicians**   ☆
★ Arthur Bliss, Joe Loss, W. A. Mozart, Nicholas Rimsky-   ★
   Korsakov, Stephen Sondheim, Andrew Lloyd Webber
      ☆ **Singers**   ☆
★ Stanley Holloway, Madonna, Cliff Richard, Diana Ross   ★

☆   **Actors and actresses**   ☆
★   Julie Andrews, Kim Basinger, Kenneth Branagh, Judi Dench, Jane
       Fonda,   ★
       Betty Grable, Groucho Marx, Omar Sharif
☆   **Media personalities**   ☆
★   Michael Aspel, Noel Edmonds, Bryan Forbes, Bob Hope,   ★
       John Huston, Bill Oddie
☆   **International celebrity**   ☆
★   Jacqueline Kennedy Onassis   ★
☆   **Sportsmen and women**   ☆
★   Pat Eddery, Nick Faldo, Bobby Fischer, Terry Griffiths,   ★
       Ray Illingworth, Niki Lauda, Diego Maradona, Pele,
       Pete Sampras

NUMBER 3

The inner conflict – opposing facets of the Number 3 personality

POSITIVE	NEGATIVE
Happy-go-lucky	Superficial
Cheerful	Frivolous
Optimistic	Naive
Generous	Easily exploited
Sensitive	Resilient
Lovable	Inconstant
Socially charming	Hypocritical
Vivacious	Ostentatious
Good living	Over-indulgent
Versatile	Unambitious
Adaptable	Changeable
Communicator	Lightweight
Quick thinker	Unmotivated
Team worker	Dislikes routine
Dutiful	Lacks staying power
Able	Easily distracted
Charitable	Careless with money
Romantic	Flirtatious
Loving	Fickle
Weaknesses	Compensating strengths

PERSONALITY

Number 3 is the final part of the great life trilogy of father, mother and child, but this does not mean that it is first and foremost a number of family, for it is Number 2 above all which signifies domestic values. Rather, in the sum 1 + 2 = 3 and the sequence 1, 2, 3, this child of numbers brings the joy of wholeness and completeness to the primary union, and those born under its influence are usually to be envied.

In adults of the number, therefore, the *joie de vivre*, happy chatter and natural curiosity of the innocent child are never too far from the surface, even if the trials of life can dull the initial, careless rapture of youth. The years may take their toll, but Number 3s always put people first and the bloodless abstractions of everyday existence a poor second. They like people best and are best with people, so it is mainly as communicators of one sort or another that they make their mark. Privately or professionally, it is Number 3s who are so often the essential catalyst in the endless traffic of human relationships.

Number 3 people are generally likeable and adaptable characters. They have a strong sense of humour and their social ease makes them popular with almost everyone they meet. Very rarely are they dull and unimaginative. They think fast, can turn their hand to most things, and are sometimes quite brilliant, especially with words, either spoken or written. If they have religious interests, it is the Church as a group of people, different and diverse like all groups despite their common purpose, not its theological aspects, that really attracts them. However serious they appear to be, secretly many Number 3s prefer social life to work, and solitude is anathema to them. Basically free spirits, both men and women of this vibration may even find family ties and their responsibilities to those closest to them a restricting influence. They are trusting, on occasion to the point of naivety, and sometimes lay themselves open to exploitation by people more ruthless than they are. But although they prefer peace and harmony to conflict, dislike arguments and are easily upset by adverse criticism, they are never down for long and have a wonderful capacity to bounce back.

If Number 3s have a fault, it lies in their tendency to be superficial. This is nowhere more apparent than in the social sphere many of them find most congenial. So their ability to amuse and entertain can easily degenerate into ostentatious display, and they can fall into the trap of trading real respect and genuine affection for cheap praise and easy friendship.

Those who are rich or successful are especially vulnerable. Generous to a fault and renowned for their hospitality, they readily attract a wide circle of acquaintances and friends, some of whom may be just the fair weather variety. But all people like to be with Number 3s and basically they do not mind being used in this way. Hypocrisy is part of the social game to them and they may not be entirely free of it themselves. Kind and sympathetic to all those drawn into their orbit, they seldom form deep, lasting friendships and can drop people just as easily as they take them up. This whimsical streak can upset others and may be dangerous if it spills over into business life.

Thus the talents of the social butterfly can be as much a hindrance as a help in career terms. Number 3s are cheerful and optimistic and fit easily into any organisation. But they frequently fail to see below the surface to the competitive nature of life and find it hard to grasp that superficial pleasantry without commitment is as much a part of business as of social life. As a result, the very hypocrisy of which they themselves are sometimes guilty in their dealings with people, may explode in their faces when the really unscrupulous types prove false friends in the fight to succeed.

Once they realise that it is dangerous to be too trusting, their natural allegiance to the group of which they are a part produces a strong sense of duty which can take them a long way up the ladder in their chosen field. They seem to do best in corporate enterprises where everyone is pulling together towards a common goal. But not many of them scale the heights. They may be just that bit too well-meaning or nonchalant. But if they are passed over for promotion and the highest positions, this is not the disaster it might be for some people. Number 3s are rarely motivated by ambition alone. So they do not worry too much if life's greatest material prizes elude them. They will always make the best of things, and even find a way to have a good time in unfavourable as well as favourable circumstances.

Most Number 3 people have a wide range of interests and like to have a finger in a lot of pies but, if they are going to find success in a big way, it will be in work where their skills as communicators are at a premium. The show-off in them makes natural actors and actresses, on and off the stage. Their ability to stimulate and entertain make the theatre, television and radio perfect outlets for their talents, whilst their way with words enables some of them to become first-rate journalists and professional authors. Fame will elude most Number 3s of course, but more ordinary careers as teachers or sales people, for example, provide the audience many of them crave. Because of their adaptability and 'have a go' approach, they are found in every occupation but, whatever the job, it will only make them truly contented if it brings them into contact with the hustle and bustle of 'the world'. Movement and change in daily life excite them. Immobility and repetition leave them cold.

Should they not fare as well in their careers as they hope, this will nearly always be because they lack discipline or endurance to a greater or lesser extent. Metaphorically speaking, they are sprinters not marathon runners and for many of them the grind of long-term hard work can be tiresome. The '9 to 5' routine, day after day, year in, year out, is most people's lot in life and the Number 3 person who cheerfully expects others to do the unglamorous chores while they avoid the routine slog can only expect to be rewarded commensurately.

Also many a promising career will go awry because of the fickle streak in this vibration. Failure to persevere when the going gets tough and a tendency to switch horses in mid-stream is typical of so many of those born under Number 3 that it sometimes seems as if these faults are second nature to them.

Often Number 3s are those who know the score but who deep down remain charming, lost children, aware of the ways of the world but ultimately dreamers or dilettantes – potential high flyers who achieve only the dubious tag of 'nearly men'. The trouble may be that these people have so many interests and ambitions that it is hard for them to achieve anything at all. They will always do best if they learn to concentrate the mind and avoid dissipating their abilities on each new whim that takes their fancy. Even those who go a long way in life seem to lack the steely determination that will carry them to the very top.

It is not surprising, therefore, that many Number 3 women are not at all career-minded. Those that are, like the men of this number, are likely to be happiest in jobs where no two days are alike. Secretary to a glamorous and dynamic boss, work involving meetings and lunches with interesting clients, jobs with the opportunity for plenty of travel and frequent changes of scene – these are ideal for Number 3 women. By contrast, boredom is a curse they will do almost anything to avoid.

Whether or not they do the kind of job that really suits them best, it would always be a mistake to underestimate working Number 3 women. They are lively conversationalists who possess more than average charm and who relate well to almost everyone they meet, but they can also be very stubborn. A witty, charming woman who will not take 'no' for an answer is a very powerful force. If they set their minds to it, women of this vibration can have very successful careers in any sphere.

Those who do not find work which really interests them are likely to opt for marriage at an early stage. Obviously marriage as an escape will not guarantee success in a permanent relationship, and any Number 3 woman who finds herself likely to take this step should stop to examine her motives very closely.

Marriage for a Number 3 career woman is more likely to happen later than sooner, and she will probably carefully weigh the relative advantages of remaining at work or taking the plunge in marriage. If someone sweeps her off her feet, she could opt for marriage without much hesitation, though she will probably try to have the best of both worlds by carrying on with her career even after the birth of children if this is at all possible.

In general, Number 3 men and women are often attracted to the glamorous types among the opposite sex, and their own social talents will give them plenty of opportunities to meet people with an exciting sexual aura. But a stable marriage needs more than glamour, and in choosing a life partner Number 3 people of both sexes should look beyond superficial appearances and rely on their knowledge of human nature to guide their actions. Like poles do not always repel in human relationships, and a Number 3 married to a staid partner who does not share their enthusiasm for an active and varied social life would, at the very least, face difficulties that might not be easy to overcome.

Number 3 men and women tend to begin by being idealistic about marriage and may view it as a wonderful event which will automatically change their lives for the better. Once they lose the romantic haze and come down to earth, they often find the old enemy, monotony, beginning to rear its ugly head. The resulting disenchantment may be a shock to their systems.

The Number 3 man will have his work as an escape route but, even so, he may find too much togetherness something of an emotional straitjacket. Fickle by temperament, he might eventually start to seek consolation in flirtations which may or may not prove harmless.

Here the difference between the sexes is instructive. The Number 3 man is not above an occasional indiscretion for its own sake. The over-riding motivation will probably be the need for variety, excitement and adventure, and may not be a reflection upon the true state of his rela-tionship – which could be perfectly satisfactory.

But the Number 3 woman will usually only deviate from the 'moral' path because of a basic dissatisfaction with her marriage. She believes that licence threatens the privileges granted to women through absolute commitment to one male. So for a woman of this number an extra-marital 'fling' is likely to be a very serious affair indeed.

Shared interests are the ultimate safety valve for a marriage involv-ing any Number 3 person. Common interests and a joint social life are the cement most likely to bind the partners into a single unit where affection and respect can be consolidated and given the chance to grow.

Any tendency to go down the path of separate interests and a different set of friends could be the first step to separate lives, frequently with disastrous consequences.

Though not exactly maternal or paternal in the fullest sense of the words, Number 3s are good with children, their own as well as other people's, though not in an over-sentimental way. To them, happy children are fellow creatures just as much as adults, except that they have more spontaneity, fun and hope. Number 3s respond to them exactly as they would to any lively companion.

Money for its own sake has very little attraction for Number 3s. They are far from being ascetics who will give away all their wordly goods as an act of faith, but they never see money as an end in itself. So they can be regarded as 'charitable' in the true sense of the world. They actually enjoy giving, just as they enjoy receiving. If, when all the sums are done, they come off slightly worse, this does not worry them in the least.

Yet they do appreciate comfort and a little luxury. So, like nearly all of us, they need cash to ease their passage through life. But, because they are cheery, optimistic souls, they expect it to grow on trees. As a result they may have to curb a tendency towards extravagance and cut their coats according to their cloth. Thrift comes very hard to them, but financial prudence is a virtue they need to cultivate even though it runs contrary to their natural instincts. Also they should be wary of get-rich-quick schemes. Their trusting natures make them potential prey for sharp operators only too willing to take advantage of it.

In matters of health, emotional upsets may cause problems as much as physical causes. The social vices of overeating and excessive drinking also present obvious dangers, but provided proper care is taken, many Number 3 people have a long life.

Given their basic character, coffee mornings, the 'local', restaurants, dinner dances and parties are where typical Number 3s are to be found enjoying themselves. If they have sporting interests, it will be the camaraderie of the changing room or the formal charm of the club dinner that they really enjoy, however much they like the game itself. Solitary pursuits are out. They are very unlikely to be found toiling up a mountain or spending long hours on the end of a fishing rod by some lonely stretch of water.

Best equipped of all people to weather the storms of life, if Number 3s had a motto it could well be 'easy come, easy go'. Success or failure, wealth or relative poverty, triumph or tragedy, the pendulum swings back and forth, sometimes close to the outer limits of its trajectory, yet Number 3s continue on their own sweet way, now up, now down, but always full of hope and optimism, and supremely aware that it is indeed a long road that has no turning.

NUMBER 3 CHILDREN

Number 3 children are neither quiet or unassuming. They are show-offs who unashamedly demand attention from parents and playmates alike.

Girls can lack the modesty they are supposed to have and will use their charm to grab as much of the limelight as they can. For all these children an audience is essential, because only through the reaction they receive are they able to give proper definition to their own inner drives as they affect their place in their world. It sometimes seems that there is a vacuum at the centre of their being which can only be filled by others. But this is not really the case. They have extremely vibrant personalities, but they can only find expression through the chemistry of interaction with other people. Ignored or isolated, they are like plants without water which will eventually wither and die.

They may be loud and boisterous when very young and there will be tantrums if they do not get their own way, so parental weakness at this stage could easily produce a spoiled brat. These youngsters should never be indulged, especially if other children are alienated by their excesses. A lonely evening or two confined to their room will be enough to show them the light, and once they have learned their lesson, they will start to integrate more successfully. Realising that self-centred histrionics get them nowhere, they will modify their behaviour and soon find that they can get on well with everyone. The older they get, the more they will discover that they like being popular, and the once wilful child should gradually emerge as a young person with a gift for mixing with all sorts.

They like school as a social stage for their outgoing personalities, but they need to be kept up to the mark in their studies. Play will always be preferable to homework, and here the discipline they cannot give to themselves may have to come from either parent or teacher.

Children of this vibration are emotionally tough. For instance, those of them born into a marriage that eventually breaks down get over it very quickly and seldom suffer any lasting damage. They will accept a stepfather or stepmother more readily than most children, while retaining affection for a lost parent, provided of course the latter is prepared to show willing. This ability to shrug off emotional trauma, whatever its cause, is a trait that characterises their early years and it will almost certainly stay with them all their adult lives.

Also they may leave home sooner rather than later, and any parent with a tendency to cling on may find themselves very quickly pushed into the background. So when the time comes, their parents should be ready to 'let go' and give such youngsters free rein to make their own mistakes in the world.

Remember that Number 3s are optimists who always look to the future. Once they fully mature, however, their sense of duty, quite apart from genuine filial affection, will lead them to give full recognition to the ties of the past.

COLOUR

Violet and shades like purple, mauve and lilac suit Number 3 people best. The combination of red and blue brought together in these colours reflects the headstrong vitality of the former and the calming effect of the latter – thus defining but at the same time controlling the tendency to impulsiveness which is a major Number 3 characteristic.

Basically the 'violet' personality always seeks to captivate. Violets are seductive. They attract people in a very subtle way, for those affected by them seldom realise their potency and fall under their spell without realising it. So exploitation of these colours by Number 3 people will enable them to charm or fascinate others, and provide the buttress to their self-esteem which they often need in moments of doubt or uncertainty.

FAMOUS NUMBER 3 PEOPLE

☆ **Monarch** ☆
★ Queen Victoria of Great Britain ★
☆ **Modern British Royalty** ☆
★ Princess Alice, Duchess of Windsor ★
☆ **Politicians** ☆
★ Indira Gandhi, Kenneth Kaunda, Edward Kennedy, V. Molotov, ★
Robert Mugabe, David Owen, John Prescott, Pierre Trudeau
☆ **First Lady** ☆
★ Hillary Clinton ★
☆ **Religious Leader** ☆
★ David Sheppard ★
☆ **Aviator** ☆
★ Amy Johnson ★
☆ **Adventurer** ☆
★ Casanova ★
☆ **Writers** ☆
★ Jane Austen, Robert Bolt, Robert Burns, Roald Dahl, Charles ★
Dickens, James Herriot, Edward Lear, Boris Pasternak,
Anthony Powell, Bram Stoker
☆ **Artist** ☆
★ Salvador Dali ★
☆ **Cartoonist** ☆
★ Osbert Lancaster ★
☆ **Designer** ☆
★ Mary Quant ★
☆ **Architect** ☆
★ Hugh Casson ★
☆ **Musicians** ☆
★ Kenny Ball, Gustav Mahler, Henry Wood ★
☆ **Singers** ☆
★ David Bowie, Fats Domino, Johnny Matthis, Johnny Ray, ★
Tommy Steele, Rod Stewart
☆ **Actors and actresses** ☆
★ Hywel Bennett, Honor Blackman, Yul Brynner, ★
Richard Burton, Jim Carey, Christopher Cazenove, Ronald
Coleman, Lesley Anne Down, Mia Farrow, Susan George,
Hugh Grant, Alec Guinness, Audrey Hepburn, Charlton Heston,
Harpo Marx, James Mason, Anna Massey, Anthony Quayle,
Jean Claude Van Damme, Julie Walters

☆   **Media personalities**   ☆
★   Peter Cook, Clive James, Spike Milligan, Harry Secombe,   ★
         Jayne Torvill, Brian Walden, Mary Whitehouse
☆   **Sportsmen and women**   ☆
★   Mike Brearley, Graham Gooch, Stephen Hendry, Gary Lineker   ★

NUMBER 4

The inner conflict – opposing facets of the Number 4 personality

POSITIVE	NEGATIVE
Worthy	Over-serious
Dutiful	Rigid
Virtuous	Sanctimonious
Conventional	Narrow-minded
Traditional	Blinkered
Conservative	Reactionary
Loyal	Reserved
Self-centred	Thoughtless
Calm	Explosive
Ambitious	Greedy
Assertive	Closed to reason
Persevering	Stubborn
Efficient	Uncaring
Dedicated	Cynical
Resourceful	Ruthless
Leadership qualities	Manipulative
Practical	Unimaginative
Hard work	Strain
Success	Materialism
Failure	Frustration
Romantic	Calculating
Sexual naivety	Disillusion
Dominant	Dominated
Supportive	Destructive
Sensitive	Reserved
Prudent	Mean
Admirable	Unattractive
Burdens	Rewards

PERSONALITY

Number 4 was, for Pythagoras, the number of true foundation and as such the most solid and substantial of numbers. This solidity is transmitted to the character of those born under its vibration. It denotes dependability, firmness of purpose and endurance. Number 4 people always stick to their guns, even to the point where their stubbornness can cost them dear. Like Number 1, Number 4 is a creative number, but Number 1 is positive and Number 4 is negative. The creativity of Number 4s is therefore cruder and more limited and, rather than bringing the mental fireworks of the original thinker, it gives the laborious logic of the intellectual artisan. Because it is much more practical it may, in the long term, achieve more in the world.

Number 4 is also the number of explosion, for the most solid base can shatter if the pressure on it is great enough. As a result the stoic calm of the typical Number 4 person may break out into anger when their over-serious natures fail to find a safety valve in stressful situations.

Tough is the key word for Number 4s. They are often physically strong, have an abundance of mental stamina and bear life's ups and downs with great fortitude. They are the true 'salts of the earth', hard-working and thorough in everything they tackle. There is nothing superficial about them, and their creativity is founded upon admirable common sense, backed up by powerful flashes of intuition. Usually they 'make haste slowly', but however hard the going gets, they press on with steadfast determination. Because they have the courage of their convictions in all they say and do, they are not easily deflected from their purpose either by self-doubt or obstacles placed in their way by others. So more often than not they succeed in their aims. It may take time, but when success and fulfilment come they will be a just reward for what may be years of unflagging application.

In their dealings with other people, Number 4s are attracted to solid, dependable characters like themselves and have no time for the frivolous or shallow. Once they have given their affection or respect to someone, however, they make loyal allies. But their earnest natures tend to get the better of them. They will ignore those they dislike as far as possible but they have a habit of subjecting associates and friends, as well as loved ones, to homilies about what is good for them. Such sermonising is no doubt well-intentioned but others may not find it easy to take. Some things are better left unsaid, and the typical Number 4 needs to realise that he or she does not have exclusive rights on how to do the correct thing.

This emphasis on what is right and proper is linked to the fact that these people are nearly always strong traditionalists. They value the solid foundations of the past and are mistrustful of the new and untried. Stability, order, convention – these are the touchstones of most Number 4s who see traditional standards as the firmest base on which to build a stable future. Whatever their place in society, they are basically 'establishment' figures who only feel at ease within the fold of respectability. But they are seldom snobs or people who indulge in social climbing for its own sake. Rather, as traditionalists, they are much more likely to set great store by their 'roots'. If they rise in the world, they generally do so with a lack of pretension that others find very disarming. It is always the straight and narrow of their own beliefs and code of behaviour which is important to them, and should they deviate from that fine line, their fall from grace is usually followed by shame and self-disgust, and a determination to get back on the tried and trusted path as soon as possible.

A big danger for such solid, conventional types is that, although they are capable of soaking up large amounts of punishment, their stoicism may sometimes degenerate into a passive acceptance of things as they are, even when they are themselves restricted or frustrated as a result. Resistant to change and reluctant to take chances, they can get into a rut very easily. Once caught in a mesh of routine and repetition, either in their external or emotional lives, they ought to give themselves a thorough mental shaking, but can find this very hard to do.

Number 4s are generally the most stable of human beings, though their public face can differ from individual to individual. They may be strong, silent types who think a lot and say little. Sometimes they are chatterboxes who hide their inner seriousness behind a stream of words. They can be quiet and self-effacing, or brash and full of their own importance, even arrogant on occasion. But they are almost always strong people who are in control of themselves, and this they communicate to others, whatever the style of their normal external behaviour.

Yet, for all this characteristic self-possession, they do not lack an emotional side. They can get very upset indeed. They want the best for themselves in every area of life, and when all is well they are warm and affectionate. But failure goes very hard with them. Cracks may appear in the control, leading to emotional outbursts – directed even at innocent people whose only offence is to be in their vicinity. So these decent, worthy souls are quite capable of fits of bad temper, often accompanied by a biting sarcasm, which they seem powerless to control. This may appear right out of character for individuals who are so exemplary in most of their conduct. This is because many Number 4s, though not fundamentally selfish, are thoughtless. They pursue their own interests with such determination that they are often blind to the possible effect their behaviour might have on others. If someone points out the error of their ways, they become defensive and feel hard done by. But in sober moments they are supremely rational and when they have calmed down and had time to think about things, they are quite likely to feel remorse and make shamefaced apologies for their lack of consideration. But by then real damage may have been done.

In their work nearly all people born under this vibration desperately want to get on. They usually set their sights very high, and are ready for almost any sacrifice to achieve their aims. If blood, sweat and tears are needed to succeed, then they are quite prepared to shed all three in large quantities. Sometimes what they do achieve does not seem to bring them much personal happiness, at least as far as outward appearances go, but that is not the point. Nor is just winning for the sake of winning the primary motivation, and they are not really looking for something so simple as a boost to the ego. The force which drives them on is much more deeply rooted in their consciousness. The real reason for all the dedicated, unstinting effort is that wordly success brings the respect of other people. In the eyes of the world, Number 4s want to be 'someone': men or women of consequence who by their own efforts have risen above the mediocre and the second-rate. They can then hold their heads up high, safe in the knowledge that they have done as well as the next person, and very probably quite a bit better. This is the kind of success they prize above everything.

Of course all the self-sacrifice and devotion to duty have their negative side. People who are driven to succeed often appear cynical, materialistic and greedy. They can be too ruthless in pursuit of their ambitions, and so appear to others self-centred and uncaring. Here appearances do not always lie.

Like Number 1 people, with whom they have a close affinity, they are not certain to be successful, but most of them have more than their fair share of what it takes to rise in their chosen field. Quite apart from their undoubted capacity for hard work, they display considerable skill in handling difficult situations. True, they are of an independent turn of mind and, like Number 1s, find it hard to admit that they are wrong about anything. But, unlike Number 1s, they are much more open to reason. If their initial reaction is always to think that their view is the correct one and to say 'no' to any suggestion that runs contrary to it, they will frequently allow themselves to be persuaded by sheer force of argument. Many Number 4s are born to lead, but they will lead through consultation and consensus that carries others with them, not by imposing their will on subordinates.

Even the Number 4s who lack above-average intellectual gifts have the ability to succeed by steady application, and they learn quickly from their mistakes. They get things done by grit and determination, even if they take a wrong turning or two from time to time. They are fighters, and they never fail in anything for want of trying.

Many Number 4 people show exceptional ability in any occupation where a practical bent is required. They like solid objects and solid problems, and are much less at home with theory. They are also good at office routines. They do not allow themselves to give in to boredom if they can make anything of a job. Even in quite humble positions, they get on with their work and never waste time in idle gossip. A lot of them do well running their own businesses – their energy and willingness to make sacrifices often pay dividends, and a successful enterprise will satisfy their basic need to demonstrate their own worth.

Sometimes Number 4 people attempt a career in organisations which attract them because of an established name and a long tradition of excellence. They may succeed here, although if they have any weakness in the work place, it may lie in their inability to function at their best as part of a team. Self-possessed and basically independent, they are happier in jobs where they can make their own running. Submerged in a large organisation, they can come to feel that their true value as employees is not sufficiently appreciated by those who matter. Once disillusioned in this way, they may become unhappy with their lot and lose the motivation needed to rise to senior positions.

Despite their self-contained inner lives, nearly all people born under Number 4 need a normal sexual relationship and family life as a main support in the battles of life. Socialising only really interests many of them in so far as it supports their business activities, and even those who do like a good time are unlikely to allow their lives to be completely dominated by a social whirl. Most Number 4s find the simple routines of domestic life neither boring nor restricting. Indeed, as people with a purpose they are perhaps more conscious than most of the importance of 'family values'. So marriage and setting up home are usually an early priority.

Such obviously reliable people are invariably regarded as good husband or wife 'material' by members of the opposite sex, and they attract plenty of sexual interest despite their rather cool exteriors. But Number 4s are seldom romantic figures, and they are not usually interested in romance or sex for its own sake. On the contrary, falling in love is nearly always a serious business for them, with marriage as the aim when they take the trouble to get emotionally involved with someone.

As suitors, many Number 4 men show a touching innocence that is strangely out of tune with their realism in business affairs and the like. In essence they are male chauvinists looking for a 'lady'. So it is not the lascivious charms of a generously endowed Hollywood screen goddess that they seek, but a Lolita-like sex object with the demure innocence of a medieval, convent-educated damsel-in-distress. Not surprisingly they hardly ever find someone who comes anywhere near so ridiculous a fantasy figure. In fact, encountering flesh and blood, they often marry for all the wrong reasons. Almost on the rebound from the impractical ideal, they may well choose, or be chosen by, women whose powerful sexual charm is combined with formidable inner strength. The latter quality may not be immediately apparent but, once married to such a woman, the typical Number 4 male, who needs to be in charge in a relationship, has difficulty in dominating her. He will try to control all aspects of her life, wanting to know her every move and attempting to dictate to her what she can and cannot do, approving or disapproving of her friends and generally censoring her lifestyle. With the wrong person this could easily produce an explosive relationship – the very opposite of what he was looking for in the search for a submissive, but highly sexed young innocent.

Alternatively, a lot of Number 4 men 'marry for money' as a way of furthering their ambitions. This may or may not produce a happy marriage. It depends if the primary motive is enhanced by sexual compatibility and mutual respect when they come to the serious business of living together from day to day.

As for Number 4 women, they are emotionally tough, usually able to manipulate others both in the sexual arena and in many other areas of life. They need to find male partners who, like themselves, have strong power drives and a great deal of ambition. If they fail to do so, they may experience frustration and even anger which could lead to them destroying their partners emotionally.

But with the right husband, a Number 4 female will work hard to further his interests. They often improve physically with age, turning into handsome, imposing women who can manage the social side of their husband's career in ways that can be of great assistance.

If Number 4 women have a weakness in their inner lives it is in their tendency to be in an emotional straitjacket. An excessive emotional response to any situation implies lack of control, and this they fundamentally dislike and distrust. They would be much more spontaneous as human beings, and probably much happier because of it, if they let their emotions run free more often, at least at times of great stress. Their relationship with their partner would also benefit from more open displays of feelings that can be seen as frank and unreserved avowals of genuine love and sympathy.

For both sexes of this number, the ideal partner is someone like themselves. The tensions which come from the conflicts within the Number 4 sexual pysche may not go completely, but two down-to-earth, practical people are stronger than one. Such an alliance, though it may not be made in romantic heaven, has the supreme advantage of providing a formidable combination for what to them is the really important thing – succeeding in life.

Whether the sexual chemistry is there or not, harmony is not guaranteed for other reasons. Number 4 people are prone to take their troubles home with them. This can cause rows and conflicts which may be 'much ado about nothing' but, if repeated often enough, can do lasting harm to family life. In general, however, Number 3s are usually faithful partners with an instinctive desire to make the best of things. They have a genuine care and regard for their children, although this sometimes becomes secondary to their wordly preoccupations.

Number 4 women may or may not be career-minded for themselves but, for all Number 4s, money is an important part of career success. Hard work usually brings financial reward, and Number 4s are very careful to make sure that they get what they regard as their fair share, even if that gives others the impression that they are just a bit too fond of it. But, though seldom personally extravagant, they do have a rather unfortunate trait of over-extending themselves financially. In business their overwhelming desire to succeed at all costs may sometimes lead them to bite off more than they can chew in financial terms. In domestic life, large bank loans and the liberal use of credit cards are temptations they should guard against. They are investors, hardly ever gamblers, and are not given to throwing their money around. They are far too conscious of the opinions of others to avoid buying a round of drinks when their turn is due, but they may suffer some personal pain when they have to do their duty in this respect.

Even if they lack the physical strength of many people born under Number 4, nearly all of this vibration enjoy good health. The real danger is overwork. They need a good laugh from time to time to take them out of themselves, but unfortunately a lot of them are just too serious-minded to indulge themselves in this way. In leisure terms, many of them have a very narrow approach to relaxation. Many like reading, but it will almost always be serious non-fiction and 'significant' novels that attract them, not a light read with an escapist yarn.

Are there any fun-loving Number 4s? Of course there are, but for them there is always a time and a place. Even those blessed with an uncharacteristic gaiety nearly always care deeply about things and lack the superficiality and frivolity of the true socialite. Business will be combined with pleasure more often than not, and work and social engagements are frequently seen as two halves of the same coin. The few *bon viveurs* among them will be conventional *bon viveurs*. The older they become the more conventional they get, as social abandon or excessive behaviour and the Number 4 personality are a contradiction in terms.

Some people may not find Number 4 persons attractive as people however much respect and admiration they deserve for their deeds in life. Yet of all the stereotypes determined by number, Number 4s are the ones who the world can perhaps least do without. If there had never been any of this number on the planet, it is a reasonable proposition that human progress would now lag far behind its present advanced level of accomplishment. Love them or hate them, the rest of us need them and what they have to offer civilised life. Their lives may not always give them great personal joy, but they will nonetheless think it all worthwhile if they have made a serious contribution, as they see it, to the society in which they lived. For so many of them this is their burden; it is also their reward and their redemption.

NUMBER 4 CHILDREN

Number 4 children are reliable and trustworthy from an early age, much more so than most youngsters. They are always eager to please and can be entrusted with quite advanced tasks early on. They love to run errands or messages and, as they grow older, jobs like washing the dishes or cleaning the car may be done voluntarily and will be a real pleasure for them. They might not expect a material reward for such help, but they will need explicit recognition of a job well done as a proof of importance in the life of the family.

In the company of other children, they will probably assume the lead in organising games and they will insist that even the most wayward of their playmates takes everything as seriously as they do themselves.

They like to do things with their hands. Give them Meccano or a train set, or a doll's house with plenty of moving furniture or some simple needlework, and these children will amuse themselves for hours.

They will need little encouragement to throw themselves into school work. Regular contact with books will probably turn them into confirmed readers for the rest of their lives, as well as giving them the material on which to cut their intellectual teeth.

The best guarantee of satisfactory development for them is a stable family life. As they grow up, they may like home life more than exploring what the outside world has to offer, so they should be strongly persuaded to go out and enjoy themselves in the company of people their own age.

COLOUR

Red, particularly its darker shades, expresses the Number 4 personality best. Through it the typical Number 4 person can bolster his or her urge for success, and its exploitation will drive them on to the action necessary to overcome competition and produce an impressive body of solid achievement. Exposure to red acts as a short-term stimulant for everybody, and for Number 4s in particular the energy and intensity it gives will be a positive help in the attainment of their goals.

Fours who favour pink as an aberration from true red may be subconsciously expressing a desire for warmth and affection. Others could be responsive to this signal, so it can be of great value in romantic situations.

On the other hand, any Number 4 who shows a marked dislike of red is likely to be frustrated or defeated in some way. There is little that can be done about this. Events will just have to take their course until the blow to the ego is hopefully forgotten as a temporary setback. The aversion to red will then most probably disappear.

FAMOUS NUMBER 4 PEOPLE

☆   **Monarchs**   ☆
★ George VI of Great Britain, Emperor Haile Selassie of Ethiopia, ★
Henry VIII of England

☆   **Modern British Royalty**   ☆
★ Duchess of Kent, Lord Linley, ★
Queen Elizabeth the Queen Mother, Duchess of York

☆   **Politicians**   ☆
★ Kenneth Baker, Alec Douglas-Home, Michael Heseltine, ★
John Major, Robert Peel, Michael Portillo, Nicholas Ridley,
Arthur Scargill, Joseph Stalin, Margaret Thatcher,
Harold Wilson

☆   **Religious Leader**   ☆
★ Desmond Tutu ★

☆   **Scientists**   ☆
★ Marie Curie, Robert Oppenheimer ★

☆   **Inventor**   ☆
★ Samuel Morse ★

☆   **Men of action**   ☆
★ Red Adair, Chris Bonington, Thor Heyerdahl, T. E. Lawrence ★
(of Arabia)

☆   **Entrepreneur**   ☆
★ Richard Branson ★

☆   **Writers**   ☆
★ W. H. Auden, Philip Larkin, John Mortimer ★

☆   **Artists**   ☆
★ Henri Matisse, Anthony Van Dyck ★

☆   **Musicians**   ☆
★ Lionel Bart, Antonin Dvorak, Yehudi Menuhin, André Previn, ★
Richard Wagner

☆   **Singers**   ☆
★ Maria Callas, Elton John, Paul McCartney, Dolly Parton, ★
Luciano Pavarotti, Sandy Shaw

☆   **Actors and actresses**   ☆
★ Jenny Agutter, Woody Allen, Claire Bloom, Catherine Deneuve, ★
Clint Eastwood, Jodie Foster, Nigel Havers, Boris Karloff,
Stan Laurel, Leo McKern, Robert Morley, Frank Sinatra

☆   **Media personalities**   ☆
★ Arthur Askey, David Attenborough, Cilla Black, Alistair Cooke,   ★
Paul Daniels, Robin Day, Roy Hudd, Angela Rippon
☆   **Sportsmen and women**   ☆
★ George Best, Steve Cauthen, Linford Christie, Joe Frazier,   ★
Sally Gunnell, Jack Johnson, Denis Law, Sonny Liston,
Arnold Palmer, Fred Truman

NUMBER 5

The inner conflict – opposing facets of the Number 5 personality

POSITIVE	NEGATIVE
Mystic	Vague
Elusive	Wayward
Active	Restless
Volatile	Erratic
Adaptable	Changeable
Curious	Superficial
Free thinker	Eccentric
Eloquent	Verbose
Convivial	Unemotional
Optimisitic	Naive
Enterprising	Inconsistent
Adventurous	Reckless
Exploration	A leap in the dark
Flexible	At the mercy of fate
Gifted	Irresolute
Independent	Irresponsible
Career potential	Career changes
'Intellectual' love	Emotional conflict
Amorous	Unphysical
Inhibition	Resentment
Insensitive	Fickle
Flirtatious	Faithful
Creative	Wasted talent
Vitality	Caprice
Search	Turbulence

PERSONALITY

Who or what are Number 5s? This is not always an easy question to answer. Number 5 people have an elusive quality which makes it hard to draw strong personality lines that apply to all of them all of the time. The traits typical of the vibration are there, but in any single individual some may be dominant at a given time, while others are hidden or in abeyance. On occasion some characteristics can seem to contradict one another. It would be wrong to overemphasise the chameleon tendencies of the average Number 5 person, but it is something to be borne in mind when seeking their deepest motivations.

Part of the problem is rooted in the fact that 5 is the least substantial of numbers. It is the middle number between 1 and 9, and often draws into its vibration people from either side of the series who have no other psychic home. It is hardly surprising, therefore, that quite a few Number

5 people have difficulty in understanding where they fit in the scheme of things.

Number 5 is the number of the pentagram or pentacle, the magical, five-pointed star of the occult which spreads out in all directions seeking consummation. This can be a star of good or evil omen, as it pulls those who come under its influence towards the untried and unexplained where the fruits of discovery stand in opposition to the dangers of the unknown. Five is not static. It is a volatile number whose endless search can create confusion and discord in human life. Only if the quest is harnessed and controlled will the properties of this number yield the plenty predicted by the original Pythagorean analysis.

Because Number 5's psychic core is ruled by searching, those born under this number are the unquiet souls of the Earth. They are not steady, reliable types who accept their lot and get on with life. Number 5s often find the routine of everyday living tiresome and are likely to go in search of some dream that could turn out to be illusory. For them, the grass on the other side of the hill is always greener. Easily bored, they are natural gamblers who are never afraid to take a chance in the hope of finding something exciting which will satisfy their restless yearnings. So they are attracted to instant panaceas and wild schemes that so frequently fail to come up to scratch.

They are interesting people to know, and they genuinely like most people, at least on a superficial level, even if their impish charm sometimes offends staider types. Possessed by an insatiable curiosity, they are talkative gossips always ready to exchange ideas and opinions with others. They may also be keen but usually unselective readers and absorb scraps of knowledge like sponges, supplemented by half-remembered truths from conversations. So they can become a mine of useless information. Not exactly the life and soul of the party, the typical Number 5 can be found in a corner at social gatherings, earnestly discussing some, to them at least, fascinating topic with anyone who is prepared to listen and respond. There may not be much substance to what they are saying, but they are never boring.

Their lively but apparently shallow temperament has obvious drawbacks. Everything is a bit of a lark for them, and their easy-going optimism can get them into all sorts of trouble – when hope and expectation turn into castles in the air, other people may take advantage of their childlike faith. Also, they tend to be highly strung and live on their nerves. This produces a capriciousness that can express itself in the form of great versatility, but it can also cause contradictions which flaw both their attitudes and actions.

Intellectually adventurous, many Number 5s can display great fluidity of thought. They are elastic in action too. This gives them an adaptability which always stands them in good stead, but equally they can sometimes lack resolution when faced with complex situations that tax their mental powers. They are not always deep thinkers in an abstract or philosophical sense – they are much more interested in the complicated mosaic of actual life. When they do embrace theories rather than facts, they tend to latch onto the ideas of others, and convert them into something uniquely their own. In this they can distort the original beyond all recognition and, if they lack real intellectual depth, they may end by debasing the coinage altogether.

So, many of them have no metaphysical leanings at all. Rather, they are always casting about for something new or different that will add interest and a new slant to their own lives. This desire to discover fresh horizons is so great that they tend to be attracted to the unconventional or eccentric. Fringe movements in politics and the arts often appeal, and they may become involved in secret or obscure sects. They love to flirt with unorthodox, even dangerous ideas, even though they may lack the inner conviction of a diehard revolutionary.

For many of them travel is very enticing, and the more exotic the destination the better. It could be more than just a couple of weeks holiday abroad once a year – they are just the sort to leave their homeland in search of a better life in some unknown country. Even when they are in a settled way of life, they flit around like butterflies from one activity to another.

Number 5 has sometimes been regarded as an unlucky number. This is not really because of any intrinsic pyschic malevolence, but the number does carry within it a lack of equilibrium which can be extremely damaging if Number 5s allow themselves to become victims of the shortcomings that arise from it. So Number 5s may suddenly go from optimism to pessimism, or from constructive thought and action to destructive, even self-destructive, behaviour. They are cheerful in ordinary circumstances but can get very low if things do not go as well as they would like, and there are occasions when their erratic tendencies make them their own worst enemies. So there will be times when it seems that they are not masters of their own destiny. Tossed by fate in the wind of life, they shift restlessly from one extreme to the other. The worst effects of this involuntary weakness will only be mitigated if they can learn the self-discipline needed to control the most volatile of their impulses.

On the positive side, they have a lot of mental agility. Their inquiring minds lead them down paths others fear to tread. Their fondness for reading makes them good at study, even though they do not always process the information gained in the most effective way. But it is their word power which is their greatest talent and their principal asset. It is also the attribute that typically distinguishes them most obviously from other human stereotypes. More than that, in large measure words define how they relate to other people and give shape to the personality which others encounter. As language is the basis for communication, this is true of all people of course, but with Number 5s the spoken word is their guiding light. Instinct and thought combine to make the engine which drives them. Yet for some Number 4s words can become an end in themselves. Instead of simply providing the tracks along which the engine runs, words can turn into the engine itself. As a consequence the typical Number 5 person gets carried away very easily by his or her own eloquence, so much so that this can override the primary intellectual impulse.

Apart from their skill with words, these people can be methodical, even analytical. But they need to be convinced in their own minds that the game is worth the candle. The slightest suspicion that they are heading up a blind alley, or that the way ahead might be excessively difficult, and they are likely to be off in some new direction.

Part of the problem, particularly in the workplace, is that they are not always comfortable with responsibility. Since they worship intellectual freedom, they can find that work imposes restrictions upon it that they accept only with varying degrees of reluctance, and the more responsible the position they hold, the more restricted they feel. So, when they begin to rise on the career ladder, they need to see this basically irrational impulse for what it is and to overcome it.

Also, they do not always cope well with problems that require judicious handling. They tend to resort to their old friends, words. But they are frequently more concerned with the shadow than the substance, and they easily fall into the trap of thinking that an eloquent gloss on the situation is all that is required, mistaking it for a real solution. So they will say things they think other people want to hear, rather than tackling the matter head on.

Another symptom of this fecklessness is the unpunctuality of many Number 5 people. If they are on time for an appointment or meeting, it almost certainly indicates that they were bored with what they were doing beforehand. If they are late, as they often are, it is a sure sign that they were fully occupied mentally and lost all track of time.

In all areas of life they do best if they can suppress their wayward streak and, at the same time, convert their power over words, intellectual curiosity and talent for easy friendship into a meaningful body of practical achievement.

When they are successful, they do well. If they fail, they are quite resilient and keep trying, but most of them need to balance their optimism with a realistic appreciation of what is possible in the short and medium term. That way the long-term future is likely to take care of itself. Many of them do come to realise this through experience, but some remain erratic to the end of their days. In almost every case middle age confers a settling influence and enables them to put a lot of the impetuosity of youth, as well as its carelessness, behind them.

Not surprisingly, Number 5s do best in jobs in which their talent for words is fully exploited. They are excellent teachers, often have a flair for selling and are well suited to jobs in the media and the world of communications. Tourism, where their interest in travel is satisfied, is another field offering a high potential for success, and many have a real talent for foreign languages which can also be put to good purpose in finding the right career.

However, for all their love of knowledge for its own sake, many born as Number 5s have difficulty in concentrating or applying themselves productively. This could hinder them in becoming a specialist in any field. Jacks of all trades but masters of none, they frequently lack the single-minded dedication to a particular line of work to rise to the top. Indeed it is not unusual to find Number 5s who have made several major career changes in the course of their working lives. By contrast the most successful of them are often people born with a special talent of no great value in the routine world which they can carefully develop from an early age to bring great success. Here the support of loving parents or of influential people who are in a position to help them can be invaluable in teaching them the discipline that will prevent them wasting their gifts.

The professional writers of this number make fascinating case studies, for in their work they frequently display the characteristics which are at the centre of this vibration. Often insatiable curiosity and a spirit of intellectual adventure find expression in a search for the undiscovered, or for meaning in the strange or unexplained. So, as authors, many Number 5s probe deep beneath the surface of life to produce writings of startling originality. Examples are the poetic visionary William Blake, who in the words of another poet, W.B. Yeats, 'beat upon the wall till truth obeyed his call', the radical scientist Darwin who shocked the world when he divined 'the origin of the species', psychic explorers such as Sir Arthur Conan Doyle, and the literary experimentalist, James Joyce. These writers truly reveal the salient force of the fifth vibration, namely the desire to seek and to find, however formidable the conventional barriers which stand in the way.

In the search for a sexual partner too, Number 5s are usually adventurous and may become romantically involved a number of times before feeling able to make a final commitment. They like to experiment in relationships and instinctively prefer to sit on the emotional fence. This tendency comes not only from that inner restlessness which gives them their liking for change and variety – it is also partly due to the fact that they find any emotional relationship other than the most casual or superficial difficult to cope with. From the time of sexual awakening onwards, Number 5 people, though on the whole at ease in the company of the opposite sex, suffer strain arising from sexual tension. This is because in serious relationships between the sexes, both the men and women seldom place the highest emphasis on the physical aspect, and in fact are frequently mistrustful of it.

So the Number 5 female is fond of the company of men. On an intellectual level she likes to share her ideas with them, and to her their preoccupations will probably seem more serious than the concerns reflected in the lighthearted chatter of other young women. But she soon discovers that sexual overtones are rarely, if ever, absent on the men's side. It is here that the tension begins, for her taste for male friendship is intellectual not physical in its origins. In maturity, therefore, she may reject male friends altogether for female.

When choosing a partner, she may be suspicious of her physical needs and select someone who can give her the mental stimulation she craves. Companionship is vital to her also but, at least in the first instance, it is likely to be based on the intellect not the senses. It is not that she rejects the physical aspect of love but that she feels that it should not be the overriding impulse which forms and motivates a relationship.

The Number 5 male is a rover. He is hard to catch and even harder to keep. Quite apart from the fact that he is always off exploring the outer edges of his world, he tends to keep women at arm's length. He prefers the company of women to that of men, whom he distrusts as sexual competitors. But his inclination is always to flirt with members of the opposite sex, not to be tied to them by emotional commitment. When he finally chooses a mate, he hardly ever confuses love with sex. For this reason even a sexually alluring Number 5 male frequently selects a plain, reliable women as a partner rather than the glamorous type everyone else expects.

For a Number 5 person of either sex the success of a marriage or long-term relationship usually depends on how far their partner understands and is prepared to accept the characteristic tendency to intellectualise romantic attachment. Fives tend to shy away from outward displays of affection or emotion. Words are much more significant to them than physical gestures like touching, hugging, kissing – and sometimes even the act of sex itself – and not everyone responds to this rather ethereal kind of love. If people of this vibration say, 'I love you', they mean it, for otherwise they almost certainly would not say it. But they may have difficulty in expressing their love in tangible form. Accused of insensitivity or coldness as a result, they feel indignant and in turn unloved themselves. As they grow older, however, they could come to realise that words alone are not enough.

When problems arise in a relationship, these people are apt to draw back from confrontation. Instead of working the difficulty through to a compromise, they can become resentful and run away from the issues, and may then form relationships with others where the pitch of emotional commitment expected is much lower. If they do stray in this way, however, they nearly always pull back should an involvement threaten to turn into a serious affair which would upset the emotional apple cart of all concerned. They are usually wise enough to see that 'jumping out of the frying pan into the fire' is no solution at all. And again, maturity may go a long way towards mitigating their characteristic unwillingness to face the emotional facts of life with their original partner.

In a stable marriage, Number 5s of both sexes make loving partners. Although they are liable to evade emotional responsibilities with a partner should difficulties arise, when it comes to children they are scrupulous in honouring the commitments imposed by parenthood. Free from the sexual and emotional tensions which exist between adults, their attitude to a child is much more open and frankly affectionate. But they are most unlikely to spoil their offspring and are seldom over-protective. They expect them to fight their own battles in life from a relatively early age.

The smooth course of a typical Number 5's family life can sometimes be upset by financial problems. Whatever their earning capacity, or that of their partner, they are not always astute where money is concerned. Clever with words, they rarely combine this with a head for figures. Even when cash is reasonably plentiful, balancing the weekly budget is sometimes a bit of a struggle. Also, though there are certainly no more habitual gamblers among this number than among any other, they can take risks where vital capital and assets are at stake. Their financial gambles may be comparatively insignificant, though sometimes they may pull off a minor coup, but Number 5s and their bank managers hardly ever see eye to eye.

In health matters, there are no intrinsic problems connected with the fifth vibration. However, because of their volatile temperaments, Number 5s tend to live on something of a 'high' and, unless care is taken, they can get run down very easily. They need to relax like everyone else, and their liking for reading can provide an excellent escape from the worries of the day. They are frequently fascinated by the media as a window on the world – satisfying their enquiring minds and thirst for knowledge, as well as providing entertainment. So Number 5s are often TV addicts, film buffs and avid readers of newspapers as well as books.

Among famous people born under Number 5 is Adolf Hitler. Cynical tyrants capable of crimes against humanity of massive proportions are not typical of any number, Number 5 included. But, putting aside the monstrous aspects of Hitler's warped personality, he displayed many of the traits of those born under his life number – in giant caricature. He was a volatile individual, a highly strung and erratic visionary with great powers of oratory, a risk-taker who was willing to gamble everything on his dreams of a Europe dominated by his country, almost as a personal escape from the drabness of his own early life. The fact that the dream was a perverted one which had dire consequences for the entire world does not make many of his inherent characteristics any less typical of those of many ordinary men and women who share his number.

Perhaps we are now in a position to answer the question which opened this chapter. Who or what are Number 5 people? Are they really so shallow and fly-by-night as they sometimes seem, especially on the surface? The answer is evidently 'no' for, of all the vibrations, Number 5 is potentially the most creative and those born to its influence have the greatest potential of all people for creativity. Their search to find a place for themselves in the world is in fact a search for a creative outlet for this enormous potential. When they find it, this is the plentiful 'harvest' Pythagoras linked so inextricably to the number.

Restless, sometimes wayward free thinkers, the world seems a dull place to these people unless they can chase a rainbow or two. If that involves an adventure or a bit of a gamble, this can be just the spice they need to bring interest and variety to their lives. Always on the move, chatting to all and sundry as they go, looking under every stone, they may not always achieve their elusive goals, although some of them find – perhaps by design, perhaps by chance – what they are searching for. Either way, the journey towards their uncertain destiny will never be uneventful. Win or lose, they will have played the game of life for all it is worth before they are finally laid to the rest they so seldom find in life.

NUMBER 5 CHILDREN

From a very early age all children are curious about the strange new world into which they are catapulted by birth, but youngsters born under Number 5 are quite exceptionally so. As soon as they can talk they will bombard their parents with a battery of questions about any topic which captures their roving interest. When they are older, however, a change takes place. They continue to ask questions, but now their preference is for learning from books, though this is not always accompanied by a liking for formal tuition. The age at which this new emphasis occurs varies from individual to individual, but it is clearly a symptom of the independence, intellectual curiosity and free thinking shown by people of this vibration in adult life. For these reasons their record at school can be patchy in scholastic terms, and a lot of these children chafe against even the quite mild discipline of a normal school regime.

This early tendency towards restlessness and non-conformity will not necessarily turn into anti-social traits later on – far from it. So the parents of such bright, energetic children have few grounds for real worry either in the present or for the long term. However, creative activities in areas that seem to particularly interest them should be encouraged as a safeguard against any inclination to squander their talents on the wide range of casual interests with which they may well flirt on the most superficial level.

Many children of this number find it difficult to relax, and fret when they are unable to unwind. They should be given their head up to a point, but care must be taken not to allow them to become over-tired as a regular occurrence. Rather than letting them burn themselves out towards the end of each day, a period deliberately set aside for relative calm is a sound idea. This habit of relaxation, instilled in childhood, will be a great boon in maturity.

COLOUR

The cheerfulness, quick wits, conversational power and social talents of typical Number 5 people are reinforced by orange. This colour may also enhance their creative capacity, for it has a cooling effect which improves concentration, and can also lessen the effects of mental or physical exhaustion and may reduce hostility or anger in times of emotional stress.

A liking for black by Number 5s is a warning light. It may be a sign that they feel they are struggling against a fate they regard as unfavourable, possibly indicating that their volatile tendency has produced a phase in which their life is out of control. The substitution of an orange for a black ambience can, therefore, have a calming influence.

FAMOUS NUMBER 5 PEOPLE

☆   **Monarch**   ☆
★   Mary, Queen of Scots   ★
☆   **Modern British Royalty**   ☆
★   Earl Mountbatten   ★
☆   **Royal Photographer**   ☆
★   Earl of Snowdon   ★
☆   **Politicians**   ☆
★   Kenneth Clarke, Robin Cook, W. E. Gladstone, Adolf Hitler,   ★
      Geoffrey Howe, Viscount Palmerston, Eva Peron, Franklin D.
      Roosevelt,

☆   **Soldier/politician**   ☆
★ Earl Alexander of Tunis   ★
☆   **Solider** ☆
★ Douglas Haig ★
☆   **Religious leader** ☆
★ John Calvin ★
☆   **Scientists** ☆
★ Charles Darwin, Galilei Galileo ★
☆   **Inventor** ☆
★ Louis Braille ★
☆   **Explorer** ☆
★ Roald Amundsen ★
☆   **Aviator** ☆
★ Sheila Scott ★
☆   **Heroine** ☆
★ Grace Darling ★
☆   **Writers** ☆
★ William Blake, Charlotte Brontë, Arthur Conan Doyle, ★
   Clare Francis, Antonia Fraser, P. D. James, James Joyce,
   John Steinbeck, Alfred Tennyson
☆   **Artist** ☆
★ Vincent Van Gogh ★
☆   **Musicians** ☆
★ John Barbirolli, Irving Berlin, Felix Mendelssohn, ★
   Gioacchino Rossini
☆   **Singers** ☆
★ Geraint Evans, Tito Gobbi, Mick Jagger, Vera Lynn, Tina Turner ★
☆   **Actors and actresses** ☆
★ Ursula Andress, Dirk Bogarde, Marlon Brando, Richard Briers, ★
   John Cleese, Doris Day, Marlene Dietrich, Clark Gable, John
   Geilgud, Joyce Grenfell, Thora Hird, Jeremy Irons, Robert
   Mitchum, Dudley Moore, Martin Shaw
☆   **Media personalities** ☆
★ David Dimbleby, Sue Lawley, Jimmy Saville, Mel Smith, ★
   Steven Spielberg, Terry Wogan
☆   **Sportsmen and women** ☆
★ Mike Atherton, Bob Champion, Bobby Charlton, Jack Charlton, ★
   Kenny Dalgleish, Virginia Holgate, Tony Jacklin, Billy Jean
   King, Olga Korbut, David Moorcroft, Ed Moses, Floyd Patterson

NUMBER 6

The inner conflict – opposing facets of the Number 6 personality

POSITIVE	NEGATIVE
Harmony	Discord
Vice	Virtue
Charismatic	Ostentatious
Image	Artifice
Substance	Shadow
Realistic	Unanalytical
Diplomatic	Manipulative
Urbane	Superficial
Conventional	Unadventurous
Love of beauty	Self-indulgent
External control	Internal conflict
Contented	Complacent
Fair-minded	Egotistical
Idealistic	Self-centred
Resourceful	Crafty
Self-seeking	Uncompetitive
Ability	Lethargy
Leader	Subordinate
Seductive	Unromantic
Attractive	Shallow
Sympathetic	Inhibited
Loving	Sexually restrained
Domestic stability	Hidden tension
Good health	Mysterious illness
Fortune's darling	Plaything of fate

PERSONALITY

Six is the number of harmony. It therefore signifies friendship, love, union, health, beauty and wisdom, and is the numerical ideal of the human condition where the sum of the parts add up to a perfect whole. As a life force it can also bring the triumph of dissolution over unity, of strife over concord, of chaos over order, and ultimately of evil over good, if the purity of the constituent parts is compromised or violated. In these circumstances only the way of truth emanating from self-knowledge and the virtuous life can maintain the perfection of harmonious influences it naturally confers. So Number 6 people must be ever mindful of the inner motivations of their psyche, and of the ethical constraints that need to be imposed upon them, if they are to reap the rewards that follow from the happy chance of having Number 6 as their birth number.

To err is human, however, and no flesh and blood creature can ever live in such a way that perfect harmony is constantly achieved either wholly or in part. Nevertheless the beneficial vibrations are so various and so intense that only someone completely at odds with their psychic balance could regard Number 6 as a number which brings them no earthly fulfilment.

Because harmony is at the centre of their being, the personalities of Number 6s may well radiate a magnetism which reflects the fact that they are, potentially at least, individuals who are a unified whole with no irregular or separate elements. 'Charismatic' is the most useful word to describe the effect this produces on everyone else. Number 6s may not be beautiful or attractive in the conventional sense, although many of them are. But whatever their natural physical attributes, they nearly all possess some sort of power which makes them stand out from the crowd.

Also, most of them know all about projecting an image, and this reinforces the power from within. Their manner, their clothes, their whole outward *persona* is carefully calculated to convey to others the impression they wish to make. They may only be half aware of how much trouble they take in order to present themselves in their most favourable light, but whether this cultivation of the external self is partly or even wholly unconscious, it certainly works. Number 6s are not the sort of people you meet one minute and forget the next.

However there is a danger, for the image may take over the real person within it, producing a basically dishonest lifestyle. Relationships with others can be dictated by the thin veneer of image and so lack true meaning, the image itself becoming so important that even when it is damaging emotionally or materially, it is virtually impossible to abandon.

The threat is greater because very few Number 6s are given to analysing themselves or others very deeply. The problems of fate or destiny, and their contribution to the unfolding of their lives, are not something with which they are really concerned. They are content to let events take their course, and they are not reflective people in the habit of speculating upon the meaning of life. Rather they are basically men and women of action, their response to people and events having an earthly quality firmly rooted in a hard-nosed appreciation of the realities of any situation. The most imaginative of them may be able to convert this realism into a unique personal view of life, but most ordinary Number 6s get on with their lives without questioning the assumptions and social norms of the environment into which they are born.

This combination of a charismatic image and a streetwise attitude to living is a very potent one. Number 6s are usually trusted, though not necessarily really liked, because of the capable image they project. This may be so even when their integrity is unproven to those who give their trust. So they are mediators and fixers perfectly placed to resolve conflicts and move things along. They make reliable confidants and willing counsellors to friends and acquaintances who seek their advice and opinions. They rarely judge people, taking them as they find them, and are tolerant of their foibles and weaknesses. They have a tendency to calculate all the angles and will rarely, if ever, be fooled by the same person twice. But the element of self-interest in their wheeling and dealing, though present, is seldom carried to excess. Sometimes they may come across as cold-blooded manipulators, but nearly all of them do in fact possess the fundamental integrity most people give them credit for.

But the calm, urbane affability which smoothes their own path in life and that of others is not the whole story. Since Number 6s almost never look too far below the surface and shy away from examining their motivations, they have difficulty in solving their own problems, even though they always seem to have a ready solution for everyone else's. They are outwardly friendly, steady, placid individuals, but there can be plenty of inner anger and resentment in troubled times. Just because their natural inclination is to hide their feelings, this does not mean that they do not exist. But Number 6s are concerned above all with the impression they have on others. It would never do to give way to displays of rage or excessive emotion which would lose them credibility as people who are invariably in control.

Hence they are excellent actors in their daily lives, but this front does not fool everybody and those who do not fall under their spell may label them cold fish with an eye only for the main chance. Perhaps Number 6s should bare their souls more, thus releasing inner tensions which can do them harm as well as winning over the minority who point to their conciliatory ways and manipulative skills as evidence of selfish double-dealing and insincerity.

Number 6 people are fond of the luxuries of life, and have an eye for beauty and beautiful things. They like entertaining, and are apt to have houses furnished and decorated as expensively as they can afford. Antiques, *objets d'art* and pictures will adorn the homes of the more wealthy – they may have no artistic talents themselves but are nearly always comfortable among fine things and creative people. They are lovers of painting, music or the performing arts in general. By contrast many of them are not great readers, preferring the concrete to the intangible.

Despite their artistic leanings, they are most unlikely to adopt a bohemian way of life. They are much too conventional for that. Nor are they adventurous by temperament. They are happiest in familiar situations and amongst people they know well. So they much prefer custom to experiment, the *status quo* to change, and all forms of eccentricity are anathema to them. When it comes to travel, it is a case of 'east, west, home is best', and the inconveniences and possible privations of faraway places are definitely not for them. In all areas of life these people need solid foundations and hate shifting sands. Any unsettling external influence is liable to upset their internal balance, and they instinctively look for danger in the untried and unknown.

Harmony implies human happiness, so Number 6 people are in the main happy, though certainly not happy-go-lucky. In fact they can sometimes appear a bit too happy for their own good. Their characteristic tendency to project an image which will impress others reinforces the general air of well-being they exude. As a result they are frequently regarded as complacent and self-satisfied by other people – and a lot of the time this may be justifiable. The belief that they, and they alone, are the centre of the universe is a failing which afflicts many Number 6s.

In any situation they tend to assume that their rightful place is always in the front row. It is when they are forced to take a back seat that their habitual contentment is most frequently shaken. Though their views are often sought by others, they are not backward in coming forward, and will offer advice whether it is solicited or not, sometimes on matters about which they have no special knowledge or privileged information. They have the manner of someone who is always right, and while this may reassure those who lack their inner certainty, it can also irritate people who are less convinced by their self-appointed mantle of omniscience.

If Number 6s have a stroke of luck they see it as no more than their due, a proper reward for their intrinsic merits. But if they suffer pain or misfortune, they are bound to consider it unfair beyond measure. Such attitudes will gain them little sympathy from less egotistical types who know that life is hard even if fortune favours them from time to time. Why should Number 6s expect a free ride? So for all their talent in handling problems and problem people, those who know Number 6 people best are among those who like them least. While they are polite and non-committal with their feathers hardly ever ruffled, they can often be very hard to take.

The extent and depth of this egotism varies from individual to individual. It tends to ebb and flow in one person according to circumstance, but it is precisely when their self-centred conceit gets out of proportion that the harmony of the vibration begins to dissolve. Number 6s are as vulnerable to internal tensions and turmoil as anyone else.

More positively, the manipulative side of the typical Number 6's nature, as well as their complacency about being members of the happy few on whom the sun should always shine, are counterbalanced by the fact that they have a real feeling about the need for fair dealing in human conduct. For all their tactical manoeuvring, they are unlikely to stoop to mean or underhand ways of achieving their ends. If they do, once again the harmony of the vibration will be broken, and they could pay the price for their reprehensible behaviour. Most of them hate to see any living thing deprived or mistreated, and though they are seldom the kind to take up causes and campaigns, they will frequently interfere when they can if their sense of decency or justice is offended.

Despite their liking for a prominent position when anything less would threaten their self-respect, work and a successful career often come second to relationships, good company and a life without too much stress and strain. This is not to say that they are all uniformly unambitious, but in a lot of cases their career does not become an all-consuming passion. The most successful of them are likely to combine a desire to get to the top with a sense of their own destiny, sometimes regardless of wordly gain. Among famous Number 6 people of the past, Charles de Gaulle exemplified these traits. In the years of lonely exile in London during the Second World War he became the personification of France and later, as the saviour of his country during and after the Algerian crisis, he pursued his high ideals with a lofty disregard for the banal preoccupations of those he saw as lesser mortals.

Such cases are not typical of most ordinary folk of this number. Many are not suited to the tough, competitive world of today. The least motivated of them can be lethargic and find the struggle of everyday life a bit of a chore, a burden to be borne, but seldom to be enjoyed. A lot of Number 6s are easily distracted and lack the drive necessary to get ahead of their fellows. If they are successful, their success is often achieved in spite of themselves, for they are frequently driven on by forces which they do not always fully understand. Also, material success is not necessarily what they truly want to be happy, especially when they find ease and contentment marred by struggle or conflict – for which they have no particular liking.

They do best when their ability to draw people to them and their taste for the finer things in life is brought into play. Advertising is an obvious career for people who set so much store by image. The hotel and catering industries, and the fashion, beauty and hairdressing trades are also excellent areas for their talents. A large number of successful business women in all kinds of commercial enterprise have Number 6 as their birth number, as they frequently possess the vital flair for people and the ability to inspire confidence which helps to get the better of male competitors. The diplomatic skills of the men, combined with their clever, calculating streak, means that they shine in any business where adroit negotiators are needed. Both sexes are at home in the world of fine arts and antiques. If they have the gifts required, the theatre – where personal magnetism is all – is made for them.

In any sort of job there are plenty of Number 6s who are not high flyers but who use their diplomatic skills to ease the way for people in more senior positions. Though never really happy away from the centre of events, they will be content with a subordinate role provided it brings them enough of the things they really value. Number 6s make good bosses too, and their scrupulous attention to fair play, as well as their charisma, enables them to command genuine loyalty from those who work for them.

Politics are a natural arena for Number 6s. Personal magnetism, the careful attention to image and the ability to manage people and events – the profile of individuals most typical of this vibration – is a perfect formula for the successful politician.

Some of the famous politicians born under Number 6 highlight the good points and the bad points inherent in the number. Charles de Gaulle has already been mentioned as a statesman with the highest ideals and we also find the socialist crusader Aneurin Bevan among them, as well as Ho Chi Minh who dedicated his life to ridding his country of French and American domination. By contrast, men like Oswald Mosley, whose fascist compaign in Britian was so misguided and such a perversion of his abilities, and Richard Nixon, who ended his long career branded a liar and a cheat, demonstrate what can happen when the harmony of the vibration is broken by the victory of vice over virtue.

In general, Number 6s are sexually attractive. But for all their charisma, they are by no means universally admired. Their ability to fascinate often creates suspicion or envy among their own sex, and in the romantic sphere there are plenty who will reject the advances of a charming Number 6 – usually the steady, down-to-earth types who distrust the glamour and who believe, rightly or wrongly, that they can see below the surface of the skin-deep sexual aura to a person who is not so attractive underneath.

For their part Number 6s generally tend to take a pragmatic view of love, with material considerations often very important in the selection of a partner. Those who see love as a potentially beautiful experience which transcends practical questions, may be the victims of their own superficiality. They allow themselves here, as in so many things, to be seduced by image. So they settle for a match which looks good to themselves and to others, but which may lack real depth. A glamorous partner, or one who brings immediate financial advantage, is a great turn-on for them, but could easily be the source of much disappointment in marriage should true compatability and genuine mutual affection be absent.

Number 6s take rejection or failure in love very hard, and become angry, even bitter, when a relationship in which they have invested time and effort goes wrong. Calculating as ever, with their characteristic tendency to dissemble, they do not always give themselves wholeheartedly in love. Therefore, in their search for a mate, Number 6 people have to learn to give affection openly and with total commitment. They will then draw to themselves a person who really loves them for what they are, not what they seem.

The importance of the sensual side of a relationship varies from individual to individual, but nearly all Number 6s like their sex clean and well-mannered – not for them the contortions of the *Kama Sutra* or the animal delights of *The Perfumed Garden*. Polite consideration of mutual needs, not unbridled passion, is what arouses them.

On a deeper level, Number 6s in marriage or a permanent relationship are often more preoccupied with smoothing things over than expressing their genuine feelings and, as they seldom say what they really mean, this can lead to misunderstanding and emotional damage.

Their careful cultivation of self-image may produce a breakdown in sympathy between partners which can go to the heart of a relationship. On the outside Number 6s are apt to try to give the impression that all is well, whatever the true state of things. This can mean that their partner fails to respond to their need for emotional empathy or support because they are ignorant of it. This lack of emotional communication is frequently the greatest weakness of any Number 6 person in a sexual relationship or a marriage. Again, they need to come out into the open and ask for love directly, not keep their feelings hidden or seek what they need in a roundabout or coded way.

In everyday living, the women shine more as hostesses than kitchen slaves, but they are good homemakers. They are sentimental, remembering every birthday, anniversary or special day in the family, and will be offended if one of their own is forgotten or ignored, at least until the wrong is righted by some peace offering. Male Number 6s are attentive husbands, at least on the surface, though inwardly they may be wrapped up in their own concerns far more than is good for an open relationship of mutual sharing. Both sexes make proud parents with a determination to draw their children into the circle of love in order to reinforce the family unit.

Financially, the main problem for the average Number 6 may stem from the need to keep up with the Joneses. So money is definitely a priority for them. They do not hanker after millions, nor do they long for fantastic luxury, but the means to purchase quality items in solid, good taste is a must. Poverty, even relative poverty, is something of a personal disaster. Extravagance is a form of self-indulgence they need to be wary of.

Number 6s are not always able to cope adequately with their own inner tensions. If pressure is allowed to build with no outlet, illness can result. Health problems that occur for no apparent reason indicate internal stress and the need for a change of direction or the formation of new habits.

However, the inability to relax is not an intrinsic weakness of Number 6s and they know how to enjoy life. They like nothing better than to entertain or be entertained by friends. Also many of them are great puzzlers. Crosswords or a game of cards in good company admirably satisfy their liking for a problem to be solved by their own resourcefulness and ingenuity.

Most Number 6s therefore do lead harmonious lives. Despite the magnetic force of the personality of many of them, they are unlikely to be shooting stars flashing across the sky of life – just solid, dependable types who have a liking for a life which is not too taxing. If they use the advantages of their birth well, they will not allow the dangers of egotism, complacency and insincerity implicit in their vibration to harm them seriously. In the hierarchy of numbers, Number 6 is on the whole a safe place to be born, even though the peace of the haven can be shattered from time to time by storms from inside and out.

NUMBER 6 CHILDREN

These children need a great deal of love and affection to provide the early emotional security on which they can build to become well-adjusted personalities in adult life. But a happy home environment by itself is not enough. They require the constant reassurance of lots of kisses and cuddles to convince them that they are truly wanted and loved, for they judge everything by outward appearances.

They are easily tempted and do not always see the difference between right and wrong when they reach out for the things they think they must have. Therefore they need to be shown the consequences of their actions in a gentle and caring way. Patient explanation and reasoned discussion will certainly be far more effective than strict, disciplinary measures. Any attempt to bribe them with presents or treats, far from showing them the error of their ways, will only confirm in them their belief that doing wrong carries no penalties in life.

Once they reach teenage, they begin to mature very quickly and may try to walk before they can run in the adult world. Whilst allowing them to make decisions for themselves and to formulate their own plans, parents can assist them by guidance drawn from their own experience of living if this is presented in an unobtrusive way. Above all, they need to learn that all the things they want will not automatically come to them, and that success and true happiness have to be worked for and earned.

COLOUR

Green is the colour of people who are well-adjusted in relation to their external surroundings with a conventional view of life. It is thus the colour which reflects most accurately the Number 6 personality at its most harmonious. Any rejection or dislike of green almost certainly indicates mental turmoil and even an uncharacteristic inner loneliness.

Number 6s are comfortable with green because it helps them to reinforce their self-esteem. It is therefore a very potent symbol for them that all is well in their world. Because they have such an affinity with it, it is also a colour they can use to support the image they wish to project either generally or on a particular occasion.

FAMOUS NUMBER 6 PEOPLE

☆   **Monarchs/Regents**   ☆
★ Emperor Akihito of Japan, Catherine de Medici Regent of France, ★
Prince Rainier of Monaco
☆   **Modern British Royalty**   ☆
★ Prince Edward, Princess Margaret, Duke of Windsor   ★
☆   **Politicians**   ☆
★ Clement Attlee, Stanley Baldwin, Tony Benn, Aneurin Bevan, ★
Rab Butler, Edward Heath, Douglas Hurd, Ken Livingstone,
Ho Chi Minh, Oswald Moseley, Richard Nixon
☆   **Soldiers/politicians**   ☆
★ Dwight D. Eisenhower, Charles de Gaulle   ★
☆   **Reformers**   ☆
★ Elizabeth Fry, Marie Stopes   ★
☆   **Scientists**   ☆
★ Albert Einstein, Peter Scott   ★
☆   **Inventors**   ☆
★ Thomas Edison, Frank Whittle   ★
☆   **Entrepreneur**   ☆
★ Bernard Delfont   ★
☆   **Writers**   ☆
★ Elizabeth Barrett Browning, Lewis Carroll, Agatha Christie, ★
Margaret Drabble, Ian Fleming, D. H. Lawrence, Iris Murdoch,
Wilfred Owen, Harold Pinter, Alexander Solzhenitsyn,
J. R. R. Tolkein
☆   **Artists**   ☆
★ Pietro Annigoni, Edgar Degas, Francisco Goya   ★
☆   **Designer**   ☆
★ Laura Ashley   ★
☆   **Architect**   ☆
★ Christopher Wren   ★

☆   **Musicians**   ☆
★   Duke Ellington, James Galway, Arthur Sullivan   ★
☆   **Singers**   ☆
★   Michael Jackson, John Lennon, Stevie Wonder   ★
☆   **Actors and actresses**   ☆
★   Peggy Ashcroft, Michael Caine, Jimmy Durante, Albert Finney,   ★
Greta Garbo, Richard Gere, Goldie Hawn, Glenda Jackson,
John Mills, David Niven, Vanessa Redgrave, Meryl Streep
☆   **Media personalities**   ☆
★   John Arlott, Billy Connolly, Charlie Drake, David Frost,   ★
Lenny Henry, Twiggy, Peter Ustinov
☆   **Sportsmen and women**   ☆
★   Bjorn Borg, Eric Cantona, Brian Clough, Trevor Francis,   ★
John McEnroe, Gordon Richards, Daley Thompson,
Terry Venables, Emile Zatopek

NUMBER 7

The inner conflict – opposing facets of the Number 7 personality

POSITIVE	NEGATIVE
Deep	Withdrawn
Private	Isolated
Introspective	Remote
Mystic	Dreamer
Wise	Intuitive
Reflective	Over-sensitive
Analytical	Dogmatic
Compassionate	Calculating
Generosity	Self-denial
Sympathetic	Formal
Honest	Uncompromising
Witty	Blunt
Conventional	Dull
Conformist	Individualistic
Cautious	Plodding
Prudent	Unimaginative
Good strategist	Poor tactician
Discipline	Freedom
Careerist	Unambitious
Romantic idealism	Emotional vulnerability
Over-protective	Dominated
Achievements	Limitations

PERSONALITY

In every occult system, 7 is the magic number. Before going any further, however, it is necessary to define this over-used phrase much more precisely if the significance of Number 7 in human life is to be properly understood.

It is not just that 7 has always been regarded as a number of super-natural power. It is also a cypher for all those aspects of the universe where simple explanations do not serve and where some element of the mysterious can be divined. The strangeness of natural phenomena, the impenetrable essence of man-made artefacts, the intangible, imperfectly understood, deepest depths of the human soul – so often it falls to 7 to delineate them by number.

There are seven colours in the spectrum and seven notes in the musical scale. Early man believed the globe had seven seas and built seven Wonders of the World to celebrate his primacy over it. Islam promises believers seven heavens of which the seventh is the state of sublime joy. The Bible warns of seven deadly sins. Seven is also a key number in the human concept of time, itself only theoretically explained in relation to space by the greatest of thinkers. There are seven Ages of Man who, within that time-scale, lives through seven days each week. The Creation itself is supposed, biblically, to have taken seven days to complete. It is no coincidence that Pythagoras, though he came from a very different religious background to either Islam or Judaeo-Christianity, regarded 7, not 9 or any other number, as the final stage of completion as we travel onward through life from the defining moment of birth.

Given the number's aura of mystery and the mysterious, it is not surprising that typical people of this vibration most commonly attract such epithets as 'dark horse', or phrases like 'hidden depths' or 'still waters run deep' to sum them up. Quiet, naturally inclined towards introspection, even introversion, to the rest of humanity they may not always seem the most well-rounded of personalities. Yet they are not really loners or outsiders. In many cases the air of self-absorption is only a defence mechanism and one which can be quite easily penetrated.

Number 7 people are liable to swings in mood, and though this does not imply that their mental balance is threatened as a result, it does mean that they can move quite rapidly from appearing remote and distant at one moment to being warm, outgoing and close to the life around them at the next. They may like seclusion more than most people, but they have little difficulty in crossing over into the hustle and bustle of the world, and are equally comfortable in either setting. In both internal and external life, the earthly existence of Number 7s will be a journey of discovery, a search for the true nature of reality as well as for understanding about their own inner selves.

Nor is it correct to dismiss them as cold or unemotional just because of their reserved manner. They are people who feel deeply and have a great deal of compassion for their fellow human beings. They may sometimes seem to find it difficult to communicate with others, but a fund of natural wisdom is at their disposal. Anyone who takes the trouble to cultivate them will probably not be met by rejection but with the relevation of a rare gift for understanding, in a warm and sympathetic way, all manner of human problems.

Nearly all people of this number spend a lot of time thinking, though they might not be blessed with the most powerful or original intelligence. They tend to arrive at conclusions as much by intuition as pure logic, but if they are basically intuitive in their thought processes, they are certainly not impulsive. They like to weigh up every situation very carefully, making a thorough mental examination of all the pros and cons before deciding on a course of action. They seldom accept things at their face value, and like to probe beneath the surface in an attempt to discover the core of truth masked by appearances.

Those who lack practicality may be dreamers who habitually fail to focus their reason or intuition in positive ways. Number 7s of this sort can be vague in their approach to the details of living, and have a tendency to drift through their days in a world of their own.

In its most extreme form this 'other-worldliness' can produce a mystic view of life which may take them along some very esoteric paths. Aleister Crowley, magician and high priest of the black arts, had Number

7 as his ruling vibration. But it is not just a hankering after the unusual and unorthodox for their own sake that can draw some Number 7 people towards esotericism. Rather it reflects the search for a fuller understanding of life's deepest aspects where ambiguity and obscurity reign, which is typical of all Number 7s in differing degrees. Of all the numbers, Number 7 is the one most likely to include individuals with clairvoyant powers, or at the very least with insights quite beyond the mental range of the average person.

Apart from dreamers and mystics, most Number 7 people are pragmatists first and philosophers second. Their quest for the deeper meaning of life remains firmly within the boundaries of a conventional lifestyle. They confine the exercise of their powers of intuition to ordinary preoccupations and problems.

In their dealings with other people, Number 7s are usually independent and display a marked individuality. Most of them may be conformists within the general pattern of their environment, but they reserve to themselves the right to go their own way within it, and automatic acceptance of the 'party line' inspired by the majority viewpoint is not their style. No one will ever put them in an intellectual straitjacket. A lot of them carry this independent caste of mind to the point where they are frank, even outspoken, and sometimes their candour stops only just short of rudeness. The fact is that they are very honest people and are liable to overlook the feelings of others in their concern for truth. However, though they usually express openly what they think and feel, they are definitely not bigots. They can see the other person's point of view, and in many cases their candid approach is tempered by a sense of fun. In lighter moments they make their views felt by a well-timed joke or pointed witticism entirely lacking in malice which can be very disarming for the recipient.

In their general attitude to life they are apt to think in terms of the grand design, and would much rather leave the details to others if they can. So when they formulate a plan, though it will be based on a thorough analysis of the underlying situation and a careful consideration of all the possible options, they do not always follow it through with total commitment. It is not that they lack the stomach for a fight should the going get tough, but they lose interest very quickly because they find the practicalities rather boring. As soon as one overall strategy has been decided upon, they are on with something else, losing sight of the fact that the original objective is still not achieved. So if things do not work out as they intend, it is frequently they themselves who must bear a large share of the blame.

Most Number 7 people are not particularly acquisitive in a material sense. True, they will defend tenaciously what they regard as their own by right, but few of them deliberately set out to acquire wealth or influence. At the same time they take a charitable view of the problems of others. Basically, they dream of a better world and will work in whatever way they can to achieve it. Were he not the stuff of legend, Robin Hood who robbed from the rich to give to the poor might well have been born under the seventh vibration. This streak of generous compassion stems from the idealism which is an essential component of their psychological make-up, and any inclination towards self-seeking will nearly always be moderated by a concern for the welfare of others. Paradoxically, however, they are frequently mean with themselves, with a tendency to forego luxuries they can well afford. Yet perhaps this is not really a paradox at all. Thankful for their own blessings, many Number 7s feel a sense of secret guilt about those who are disadvantaged in some way. Hence their refusal to over-indulge their own whims and fancies.

In addition, most Number 7s have a conscientious and highly disciplined attitude to life and work. In the daily business of earning a living this is their greatest strength, but it may also be a weakness. Their highly developed sense of duty and honesty of purpose can make them a little too rigid for their own good in a world that constantly requires compromise to make progress possible. They tend to lack the flexibility of mind and attitude needed to thread their way through complex situations where there are many more grey areas than simple choices between black and white. They are in the habit of coming right out and saying what they think when a little tactful diplomacy would accomplish far more. Their best chance of material success lies in controlling their leaning towards the dogmatic, whilst utilising to the full their analytical sense and the ability to divine the true motivations of other people.

Also, they are most likely to win through by patience and dogged determination. A dazzling coup or the brilliant exploitation of the main chance is not for them. By the time they have completed their painstaking appraisal of all the angles, the half-open door to a golden opportunity will probably have slammed shut. Even when they do realise in good time that a unique opportunity beckons, by temperament they are disinclined to risk all on a single dramatic throw of the dice.

Nonetheless Number 7s have a shrewd business sense. This can be applied in any field, but they have a penchant for travel and a deep interest in distant places. Jobs in foreign enterprise, or travel and tourism are highly suitable for them. And with their sympathetic and caring natures, they could have a vocation for the caring professions. Work for charity, the disabled or disadvantaged – whether paid or voluntary – could have a special appeal for them.

Some Number 7 females can be very aggressive when it comes to a career. The home is important too, but job success and the money it brings gives them the chance to go out and widen their horizons.

By contrast many men of this vibration lack real ambition. Their self-discipline and conscientious approach will take a lot of them a long way in life, but their independence of mind frequently lands them in hot water and can act as a brake on their progress. No respecters of persons, they are likely to come into conflict with authority figures who may be in a position to determine their future, and they sometimes feel that work in general restricts the freedom of thought and action to which they attach so much value. This is a character weakness many Number 7 men need to overcome in their attitude to work and a career.

In matters of love, male Number 7s usually display great sensitivity, and curiously enough this may hamper them in their search for a partner. It all depends on the woman of course. Most women, though they appreciate gentleness and consideration in a relationship, are also motivated to some extent by rational and material factors in their attitude to love and sex. But many Number 7 men have an intuitive approach which is all feeling and which drives practical considerations from their minds. Not every modern woman will respond to an emotional onslaught devoid of reason. They may find a grand passion divorced from the realities of a material world somewhat artificial or overdone.

Therefore, males of this vibration need to be more realistic, even matter of fact, in matters of love. They should work up to, not start on, a highly charged emotional peak in a sexual relationship. If they begin badly with a woman they lose confidence rapidly and become awkward and ill at ease, making matters worse. If they start well, they usually continue well, because once their highly emotional gambit is accepted, their practical qualities emerge as they become more sure of themselves.

Number 7 women in courtship tend to give a great deal, but also demand a great deal in return. They put a very high value on what they have to offer, which may not be equally valued by the object of their affections who accordingly does not respond in kind to their needs. As a result a lot of women of this number may not always find a partner easily. They may settle for a quiescent male who has much less determination than themselves but who is willing to comply with their demands. Not naturally dominant, the Number 7 woman may find herself leading in a relationship when in fact what she really wants is to be placed on a pedestal.

A Number 7 male on the other hand, who is so sensitive where love is concerned, may meet someone much less emotional than himself who appreciates his highly romantic approach in the short run, but who ultimately takes their man in hand and uses his sensitivity to establish the dominant role for herself. So Number 7s, like Number 2s, may 'marry their mothers' in a metaphorical sense. However, whereas most Number 2s are seeking the protection enjoyed in childhood, Number 7s can be drawn into an alliance with someone who has more emotional steel than themselves.

In marriage, the Number 7 man needs a lot of affection, as well as the guidance of a strong woman. This is true even if, outwardly at least, he is a pretty tough character himself. If his wife or partner supplies the strength but not the affection, he may look for the latter elsewhere. But he will do so without conviction. Secretly he hopes to be found out, and may be deliberately indiscreet to the point where this becomes a near certainty. If his partner becomes angry or bitter as a result, this will prove to him that she cared all along. Obviously this is a situation full of danger, for a strong woman confronted by infidelity may not be prepared to forgive and forget.

Women of this vibration are likely to be over-protective in marriage. They may seek to gain love by controlling their partner, interfering between him and his male friends, even in his business affairs – all with the general aim of running his life for him. This is clearly a prescription for possible disaster, for the man may end by rejecting such controls, and ultimately the love that inspires them.

For all these reasons any relationship involving a Number 7 person of either sex needs a lot of hard work to keep it on an even keel. This can be because it is most likely to be an alliance of opposites – a sensitive Number 7 male with a much less emotional woman, or a strong Number 7 woman with a man who allows her the emotional upper hand. Therefore a marriage of two Number 7 people will at least be one where each partner complements the other, and has a sound chance of bringing happiness to both of them.

Both sexes of this number have a healthy sex drive, but they are much more likely to be ruled by the emotions than the senses. Naughty but nice is how they like their sex, and physical love will probably become relatively unimportant much earlier in life than with many people.

It is their characteristic loyalty and sense of duty, in addition to shared interests and a very committed attitude to children, that will really help a marriage with a Number 7 person to succeed. In particular, both men and women born under Number 7 frequently establish exceptionally strong ties with their children, something usually reciprocated. They rarely make the mistake of spoiling or over-indulging their offspring, but they take their parental obligations very seriously and are prepared for almost any sacrifice in the interests of the well-being of the family unit and the happiness of their children.

Number 7, though the magic number, is not necessarily a lucky one. There is no guarantee that Number 7 people will escape the financial ups and downs which most of us experience from time to time. So it is as well that most of them are careful where money is concerned. 'Blue chip' investments and cast-iron savings plans that produce steady but reliable returns suit them best. They will do well to avoid speculative ventures offering high yields but accompanied by a high level of risk, even though they may be tempted from time to time by the prospect of a financial coup, contrary to their own natural inclination and better judgement.

Number 7s enjoy good health in most cases and have great potential to live to a ripe old age. But there are many ways to abuse or take risks with personal health, and excess in any obvious danger area should clearly be avoided. Also, ill health can sometimes result directly from emotional problems.

Sevens are fond of the outdoors for relaxation, and sport greatly attracts them. They may be quite fanatical either as players or followers of the game or activity they like best. All sports have an element of drama and glamour which offers an ideal form of escapism for them.

They also like reading. Biographies and autobiographies satisfy their urge to understand human beings as deeply as possible, and books about historical mysteries or strange phenomena are also of particular interest. In fiction, 'whodunnits' also allow them to indulge their liking for a mystery and offer them a chance to use their powers of intuitive analysis.

In general, people of this number are eminently sensible types. They make few serious mistakes in life, although they are sometimes vulnerable in matters of the heart and do not always get as much fun out of life as they should. The tendency to be over-earnest is never far away, even though they are good company and have a wide range of interests and a sense of humour. Retiring, reflective individuals they may be, but life has a way of not passing them by and in most cases they try to do a lot of things they consider worthwhile and rewarding. Fortunately for them, there is rarely any fatal flaw in their character which might eventually affect their spiritual or material happiness. In fact, of all the numbers, Number 7 is most likely to bring a life of quiet, steady achievement and inner contentment.

NUMBER 7 CHILDREN

Most Number 7 children have sympathy and concern for others, combined with innate good sense, far beyond their years. Though they are dreamers who often escape into a fantasy world in play and in solitary moments, they are usually happy youngsters. Also, because they are essentially good children with a sweet temperament and a pleasant manner, they bring much happiness to their parents. It is very easy to spoil such well-behaved boys and girls, and any temptation to do so should be resisted.

They may not be brilliant at school and may have difficulty in getting down to the study of essential subjects in which they have no special interest. But the disciplined approach which will be so evident in adult life should pull them through most scholastic problems and enable them to emerge as competent all-rounders who will be a credit to themselves and their parents.

The best advice for parents of these children is not to worry about them too much. They are unlikely to give any real cause for concern, and any wayward or dreamy tendencies will almost certainly be ironed out by the broadening of experience that comes with the years. However, in the light of their general leaning towards introspection, they should be actively encouraged to bring their feelings into the open. Here parents can help by watching closely for any unspoken worries which frank discussion may alleviate.

COLOUR

As basically private individuals who feel the need for a mechanism to protect themselves from the harsher aspects of external reality, Number 7s will find grey a colour that harmonises very well with their personality and their deepest motivations, many of which they instinctively prefer to hide. Not exactly the colour of non-involvement, it does enable those who exploit it to keep the world at a distance they find acceptable and manageable.

A preference for black over grey, however, is a sign of revolt against an unhappy phase in life. Here the natural instinct of Number 7 people to retain a measure of detachment has become an unhealthy desire to cut themselves off entirely from normal contact with spontaneous life.

FAMOUS NUMBER 7 PEOPLE

☆   **Monarchs**   ☆
★   Edward VII of Great Britain, Elizabeth II of Great Britain   ★

☆   **Modern British Royalty**   ☆
★ Princess Diana, Duke of Gloucester ★
☆   **Politicians**   ☆
★ George Bush, James Callaghan, Winston Churchill, ★
Edwina Currie, Anthony Eden, Hermann Goering, Rudolf
Hess, Saddam Hussein, Ramsay Macdonald, Harold Macmillan,
Golda Meir, John Smith, Harry S. Truman
☆   **Soldier**   ☆
★ Bernard Montgomery ★
☆   **Religious Leaders**   ☆
★ William Booth, Robert Runcie ★
☆   **Scientist**   ☆
★ Stephen Hawking ★
☆   **Engineer**   ☆
★ Isambard K. Brunel ★
☆   **Astronaut**   ☆
★ Buzz Aldrin ★
☆   **Heroes**   ☆
★ Douglas Bader, Leonard Cheshire ★
☆   **Writers**   ☆
★ Kingsley Amis, John le Carré, Jilly Cooper, Emily Dickinson,, ★
Gerald Durrell, Arthur Miller, Marcel Proust, Harold Robbins,
Dylan Thomas, Anthony Trollope
☆   **Artists**   ☆
★ John Constable, Paul Gauguin ★
☆   **Designer**   ☆
★ Hardy Amies ★
☆   **Musicians**   ☆
★ Leonard Bernstein, Eric Clapton, George Gershwin, Franz Liszt, ★
Peter Tchaikovsky
☆   **Singers**   ☆
★ Petula Clark, Adam Faith, Freddie Mercury, Dusty Springfield ★
☆   **Dancer**   ☆
★ Margot Fonteyn ★
☆   **Actors and actresses**   ☆
★ Dora Bryan, George Cole, Wendy Craig, Gerard Depardieu, ★
Bo Derek, Michael Gambon, Mel Gibson, Bob Hoskins,
Deborah Kerr, Marilyn Monroe, Roger Moore, Julia Roberts,
Peter Sellers, Emma Thompson, Susannah York
☆   **Magicians**   ☆
★ Aleister Crowley, Uri Geller ★
☆   **Media personalities**   ☆
★ Bob Geldof, Jeremy Isaacs, Derek Jameson, Ludovic Kennedy, ★
Selina Scott
☆   **Sportsmen and women**   ☆
★ Muhammad Ali, Willie Carson, Henry Cooper, Steve Davis, ★
Jim Laker, Sandy Lyle, Lester Piggott, Bryan Robson

NUMBER 8

The inner conflict – opposing facets of the Number 8 personality

POSITIVE	NEGATIVE
Self-reliant	Isolated
Intense	Cheerless
Reserve	Alienation
Haughty	Misunderstood
Practical	Unintellectual
Honest	Outspoken
Dutiful	Over-conventional
Fair	Self-seeking
Purposeful	Obsessional
Determined	Stubborn
Stamina	Strain
Covetous	Envious
Ability	Integrity
Leader	Tyrant
Powerful	Ruthless
Achievement	Insecurity
Sense of destiny	Ill-fated
Past joys	Future sorrows
Shy	Demanding
Restraint	Control
Physical inhibitions	Sexual vanity
Successful	Joyless
Affluence	Self-congratulation

PERSONALITY

In the European tradition it is the balance in a pair of scales that represents the ideal of even-handed justice, but for the ancient Greeks the number 8, dividing as it does equally into 4 plus 4, or 2 plus 2 plus 2 plus 2, performed the same symbolic function. Modern numerology focuses on the dual essence of the number, reflected in the fact that it is formed by standing one circle on top of another. So in the rhythm of time, if Number 7 is the number of completion and Number 9, as we shall see, the number of rebirth, the two halves of the cyclic 8 constantly spin back and forth between degeneration and regeneration. In this way it epitomises the transience of all human concerns as the wheel turns through longing and struggle to death and decay, with an after-life as the final, tenuous hope of ultimate redemption. Above all, Number 8 controls the fluctuations between earthly success and earthly failure in the lives of all men and women.

Number 8s are usually self-confident and self-reliant people who depend on their own inner resources to convert their aspirations into tangible reality. Whereas others curry favour, trim their sails to the wind or even back away altogether from dangerous situations, individuals born under Number 8 make their own way in life without fear or favour, always pressing ahead in their deeply held conviction that theirs must be the right path to follow. They never shirk an issue and are not afraid to speak their minds, even at the cost of upsetting others.

Never flashy or capricious, they are solid, tough and dependable. Always needing to be seen to do the right thing, for most of them duty is the concept which governs all their actions: duty to employers, to family, to friends, but above all to themselves – they will do almost anything to avoid being placed in a position where they are personally diminished by having to let someone down or are forced to betray an idea or a belief they consider worthy of support.

They are eminently practical and down-to-earth people. Daydreams and fantasies have no part to play in their approach to life. Their attitudes, plans and actions are invariably firmly rooted in a keen awareness of what is possible. This strong practicality is frequently accompanied by above-average mechanical ability and they are likely to be good with their hands, even if a lot of them have the intelligence to tackle more purely intellectual problems and pursuits.

Yet all these sterling qualities have their negative side too. People who are so utterly convinced of the rightness of what they think, say and do run a grave risk of being held back by a rigid, stubborn attitude to everything that goes on around them. Worse, many of them are hardly, if at all, aware of the dangers implicit in this rigidity. They are of course no more infallible than any other human being, but if they choose a doubtful course, they will cling to their initial view of things, even when common sense and events say otherwise. This inability to bend or give way in the face of all the facts is a weakness in their make-up that can have unfortunate, sometimes disastrous, consequences both for themselves and for others involved in any enterprise with which they are associated.

But, though they cannot bear to admit that they are wrong, Number 8s have busy, alert minds. New ideas attract them, particularly ones they can turn to their own advantage. However, in accordance with their practical bent, philosophical speculations or fanciful notions are not for them. Should they have religious leanings, they rarely swallow the tenets of a dogma without question and always look for proof. This makes matters difficult for them, as articles of faith are by definition unprovable or unknowable. Even the professional churchmen among them are seldom fanatics, combining religious belief with a strong dash of realism and an awareness that their Church must interact with the world. Number 8s in general are not candidates for sainthood. Dutiful and even-handed they might be, but saintliness and philanthropy are qualities only found among the rare exceptions of the vibration whose sense of personal duty and desire for justice in human affairs takes the form of a compassionate concern for others exercised in active ways. Most Number 8 people are much too worldly for that kind of selfless humanitarianism.

One odd quirk about the cast of mind of many people who have this number is their tendency to dwell on the past. This does not only involve a strong interest in history, from which they may try to discover truths valid for themselves, it also embraces a sentimental attachment to previous happenings in their own lives. Here too they will seek to analyse key events and personal turning-points in an attempt to formulate lessons for the future. But even on a purely nostalgic level, the recollection of happy times in childhood or memories of family now departed provide for them a sense of continuity with the past strangely at odds with their fiercely pragmatic, forward-looking natures. Perhaps in this they are subconsciously searching for ways to project transient moments of joy or intense feeling into the future as a way of enriching their lives.

In their dealings with other people, Number 8s are sound judges of character and have an awareness of the feelings and needs of others, though they may not always give them due consideration in the actions they take. So on the whole, with their deep intense personalities, many Number 8s appear cold, undemonstrative and indifferent. If they have a sense of humour at all, it will probably be of the sardonic kind. Sometimes a pessimistic streak comes to the surface. They also tend to pursue their goals at the expense of personal relationships. For these reasons, though other people may respect them, not everyone will take to individuals who are so self-assured and so much in outward control of their emotions. To be fair, however, part of the problem is that Number 8s are easily misunderstood. Many of them are not fundamentally cold, but they do hide their feelings and give the impression that they do not care what others think of them. As a result their sense of loneliness and alienation, already fixed deep in their consciousness, may be increased when others fail to respond to their lack of external warmth. To break this vicious circle, the typical Number 8 needs to be much less critical and less suspicious in their human contacts and learn to share their emotions. Otherwise there is a real risk of an emotional void being created at the centre of their existence. If they fail to break down these self-imposed emotional barriers, they can become embittered and hostile – gaining a reputation for haughtiness, or even sarcasm and rudeness in their general demeanour.

Number 8s always stick to their moral guns and many of them are also physically brave. For this reason they frequently like dangerous sports. Almost all of them are fascinated by the great outdoors. The power and magnificence of nature at its most elemental exercises a special pull.

By and large, Number 8 is not a particularly fortunate number. Not even the happy-go-lucky emerge from the trials of life unscathed, but Number 8s, who feel so deeply and care so much about the things they value, often face great humiliations and sorrows in the course of their lives, however outwardly successful they become. They may have brains, beauty, wordly power, even wealth and acclaim, but for all that, in F. Scott Fitzgerald's phrase they are sometimes 'the Beautiful and the Damned' of this world who, though they seem to have everything, may suffer many hidden privations at the hands of fate.

Number 8 people are ambitious in every sense of the word. They covet status, money and power. They are the sort who are always the first to arrive at the office and the last to leave. Nothing is too much effort if they are able to achieve the success that is so important to them.

In this they have a lot going for them. Quite apart from their capacity for hard work and their ability to sustain it, they are efficient and innovative with keen powers of perception. They could have genuine executive ability, nearly always make good organisers at any level and are excellent managers of people and events when they acquire the necessary status. Although their dedicated approach comfortably embraces routine and detail, they are sound planners who excel at conceiving long-term strategies; they are not afraid to think in terms of the big schemes which may carry elements of risk but which enhance their position immeasurably when they work. Number 8s are always very good bets to finish well ahead of the field in the career stakes.

As bosses they tend to be a bit slow, even boring, but they are not afraid of difficult decisions, and act swiftly when necessary. One of their biggest assets is that they recognise the value of teamwork and have the ability to delegate judiciously, which is the hallmark of the true executive.

With their finely tuned commercial instincts a lot of Number 8 individuals rise in the world of high finance and big business. Or they may figure prominently in executive positions in large corporations. Given their tremendous drive, they often make a go of small businesses. Their practical abilities and mechanical talents make them especially suited to work in engineering and heavy industry at all levels of responsibility.

It is not unusual to find the women of this number in occupations which have traditionally been regarded as the province of males. Many of them have the tough-mindedness and stamina to succeed in a man's world.

Artistic people born under the eighth vibration are the exception rather than the rule, but those with creative talents usually show great dedication and professionalism in the exercise of their art. Dilettantes they most certainly are not.

Yet there is another side to the success achieved by many Number 8s of both sexes in their careers. Discipline and hard work come easily to them, but they are prone to expect the same standards from others – who are not always as dedicated and committed as themselves. Here they need to get things into perspective. People will respect, even admire, someone who is strong and successful, but they will only serve unwillingly a tyrant who is ruthless and unbending in the regime he imposes on subordinates. Most Number 8s who have done well are over-conscious of the position they hold and, although they are seldom pompous about it, may become intolerant of the human failings of others. So they run the risk of abusing the power they have earned.

Many Number 8s are insecure in their achievements. However strong their position, they have a tendency to feel threatened in a way incomprehensible to individuals with less intense natures. Far from resting on their laurels, they may develop a paranoid streak, so that success brings doubt and fear rather than the happiness it would be reasonable to expect. The workaholic ceaselessly engaged in a battle to safeguard the gains of a lifetime can never be relaxed and carefree.

Instead he or she becomes habitually suspicious of, and even hostile to, the world.

Not everyone born under Number 8 is an automatic winner in life in material terms. A weak Number 8, though coveting money and success, may be afraid to take the risks involved in making it to the top, or lack the self-confidence needed to acquire just a moderate share of the superficially good things in life. Such persons inevitably feel limited and dissatisfied when they have little to show for their labours. As a result they may feel cheated by a world which they think has never understood or appreciated what they have to offer. Envy and bitterness can then cloud their judgement, thus making their predicament that much more unbearable and more difficult to resolve.

Even the people of this vibration who have the toughness to get on in a competitive world may ultimately fail. All Number 8s are in a hurry to get ahead, and here it can be a case of 'more haste, less speed'. Cutting corners is no certain formula for success, especially if it involves using people. All Number 8s have to learn patience in their desire to succeed. If they can earn a coveted position through application and hard work, they will be happier and more fulfilled than if they gain it by unscrupulous or devious means.

Where love is concerned, Number 8s often find themselves swimming against the tide. In courtship a lot of them are apt to demand commitment from a potential partner before they will unbend themselves and give free rein to their own emotions. This can produce a deadlock which makes it difficult for them to find a mate for life. Also, some Number 8 women are unsure of their own femininity and need a great deal of encouragement and coaxing in their emotional relations with men.

If, however, Number 8s of either sex do make an early marriage, a great deal of forbearance may be required on the part of their partners, for typical Number 8s are usually preoccupied at this time with work and their burning ambition to get on in the world. In these circumstances they may damage a relationship at a critical, early stage. Later marriage really suits both men and women of this number best. By then they should have progressed in their work, and time should have changed them to the extent that they are able to give more in the emotional sphere than in their youth.

A Number 8 woman needs to forge an emotional bond with a man who is governed by the same kind of power drives that she is. If he lacks the ambitious, aggressive instinct that she admires, she may end by rejecting him altogether through frustration or bitterness.

The Number 8 male, on the other hand, needs to feel in control. This may threaten his own emotional security when carried too far. Complete domination over someone else is almost impossible to achieve, and the male who attempts it even partially may fail, thus damaging his capacity for love as well as alienating his partner.

On the whole, given the right partner, people of the eighth vibration make loyal, loving mates, even if they do sometimes create emotional boundaries in a relationship. They have a liking for keeping their lives in tight, neat compartments – work, play, even love – each has to be clearly separated, with the boundaries between them clearly drawn. This may produce squabbles or emotional trauma with a partner who looks at the relationship as a whole. Certainly, many Number 8s are apt to neglect their marriage for their careers, not just in the early years, as already noted, but throughout life.

Not exactly prudes, a lot of these people can be rather inhibited sexually. Some even find sex a bit of a chore, but those who do like physical love for its own sake can be wonderful lovers with the right person. Also, quite a few Number 8s, when they are successful, view sex as a sort of reward for wordly achievements. This may cause them to look for lovers outside marriage in order to feed their sexual vanity. Here again the desire to compartmentalise important areas of their lives is evident, with a wife and a mistress fulfilling different but complementary needs. Involvement in such love triangles threatens the stability of any marriage.

Number 8 wives who have given up a career for marriage are usually dutiful partners who put their husband first and their own concerns second. They will be excellent mothers to his children and provide a comfortable, secure home for him. However, they do expect to be well provided for, and if material comforts are limited, this will be a source of aggravation, for they may not forgive a man who has failed to come up to expectations in this respect. On the other hand, many women of this vibration, unfortunate enough to be caught in a relationship where real love is absent, are prepared to overlook this if money and status are forthcoming.

Both male and female Number 8s see money as a priority in life. A successful career will not be counted a success if it fails to provide adequate financial rewards. Lack of resources will certainly cause frustration and could poison domestic life much more than would be the case with most people. But whatever their financial circumstances, Number 8s are normally very adept at managing resources and invest surplus cash wisely and well.

The best advice that can be given to any person born under Number 8 is that they should try to enjoy life more. They nearly always have the intelligence, discipline and health to achieve their aims in life, but unless they can control the obsessional streak which turns everything they tackle into an oppressive duty, demanding total commitment and unremitting toil, they may never be truly happy.

On the other hand, this portrait of the typical Number 8 person may be too bleak a picture. Can Number 8s really be so deadly serious in all they do that there is no joy at all in their lives? There is joy, even if it can be hard to discern from the outside. Number 8s get their kicks from a job well done, from a pound earned, and from climbing onto the next rung of the career and status ladder. The pleasure they get is not the arid pleasure of a Scrooge revelling in his wealth and the power it gives him over the less fortunate. Number 8 people are not monsters, just honest straightforward souls who get quiet satisfaction from the fruits of all their hard work. Money and influence bring comfort, ease and social standing, and they have a liking for the good things in life. So in their private moments they are sure to give themselves a metaphorical pat on the back, perhaps accompanied by a secret chuckle at how well they have done. Even those who do less well have the capacity to develop compensations in other directions.

As they grow older, Number 8s mellow. With the ambitious instincts blunted by the passing of the years, they are able to relax more and have more time for the leisure pursuits they like best, for they have as much capacity for enjoyment as anyone else. Children can be a great joy in their mature years, both for the men as well as the women.

So Number 8s are what they are and, if they choose to go their own way, who can say that this is not the way for them. Number 8 people have a destiny like anyone else and it could be that they are best left to pursue it, whatever joys or sorrows it may bring. Of all human types, these people perhaps know most clearly of all what they want out of life. They are also the least likely to deviate from the path they choose for themselves. Win or lose, they are prepared to take responsibility, including responsibility for their own actions, and this is the quality above all others which determines their ultimate fate.

NUMBER 8 CHILDREN

These youngsters are energetic and playful, but may lack spontaneity in their dealings with people their own age. So unless their tendency to keep themselves to themselves is corrected as far as possible early on, they could emerge as lonely and isolated in their later, more formative years. If parents also find themselves confronted with a lack of external warmth, they should never make the mistake of taking their child's involuntary defensive barrier for rejection. The constant reassurance of frank and open displays of affection may be the best way of coaxing particularly withdrawn Number 8 children out of their self-protective shell.

Number 8s usually do well at school, whatever their scholastic abilities, because they feel at ease in a disciplined environment governed by rules. Even if they are not exceptional academically, they will be able to make a worthwhile contribution in many areas of school life, and they revel in an atmosphere of friendly, and perhaps not so friendly, competition with their peers. Tough little individuals, many young Number 8s excel at sport.

As they enter the teenage period with its greater freedoms, they will begin to wrestle seriously with the greatest problem they have to face in life. This is their need to find emotional security in the context of making their own way in the world as independent people with something to prove to themselves – and to everyone else with whom they come into contact. How they handle this may determine much of what happens to them later on. They may tend to try to grow up too quickly, and their parents can help them by encouraging them to move to maturity in a measured way that will give them time to assimilate the many lessons late adolescence can teach about the art of living.

COLOUR

Dark shades, particularly of red and green, are those which most closely reflect the personality of typical Number 8 people. However, if they make a deliberate effort to escape the more sombre hues, exchanging them for lightness and brightness in their dress and surroundings, they will certainly benefit from the emotional release brighter colours bring. This will help, at least to some extent, to bring down the emotional barriers they instinctively erect around themselves.

FAMOUS NUMBER 8 PEOPLE

☆ **Monarchs** ☆
★ Emperor Hirohito of Japan, Mary I of England ★
☆ **Modern International Royalty** ☆
★ Princess Grace of Monaco, Princess Michael of Kent ★
☆ **Politicians** ☆
★ Paddy Ashdown, Jacques Delors, Michael Foot, Gerald Ford, ★
John F. Kennedy, François Mitterand, Abdel Nasser,
Enoch Powell, Boris Yeltsin
☆ **Sailor** ☆
★ Karl Doenitz ★
☆ **Religious Leader** ☆
★ Pope John Paul II ★
☆ **Scientist** ☆
★ Bernard Lovell ★
☆ **Inventor** ☆
★ Orville Wright ★
☆ **Explorers** ☆
★ David Livingstone, Captain Scott ★
☆ **Entrepreneur** ☆
★ Lew Grade ★
☆ **Writers** ☆
★ Jeffrey Archer, Enid Blyton, Rupert Brooke, John Galsworthy, ★
Graham Greene, Rudyard Kipling, George Orwell, Anna Sewell,
Tom Sharpe, George Bernard Shaw, Oscar Wilde, William
Wordsworth
☆ **Artists** ☆
★ Michelangelo, Jan Van Eyck ★
☆ **Musicians** ☆
★ J.S. Bach, Hector Berlioz, George Harrison, George Solti, ★
J.P. Sousa, William Walton, Bill Wyman
☆ **Singer** ☆
★ Bob Dylan ★
☆ **Actors and actresses** ☆
★ Anthony Andrews, Warren Beatty, Joan Collins, Joan Crawford, ★
Larry Hagman, Rex Harrison, Derek Jacobi, Gene Kelly,
Joanna Lumley, Liza Minelli, Paul Newman, Laurence Olivier,
Gregory Peck, Elizabeth Taylor
☆ **Media personalities** ☆
★ Michael Barrymore, David Bellamy, Anne Robinson ★

☆ **Sportsmen and women** ☆
★ Mario Andretti, Severiano Ballesteros, Donald Bradman, ★
Frank Bruno, Zola Budd, Jack Dempsey, Frankie Dettori,
Brendan Foster, Alex Higgins, Imran Khan, Nigel Mansell,
Jesse Owens, Mary Peters, Mark Phillips, Barry Sheene,
Lee Trevino

NUMBER 9

The inner conflict – opposing facets of the Number 9 personality

POSITIVE	NEGATIVE
Active	Rash
Vitality	Restlessness
Enthusiastic	Impulsive
Instinctual	Accident prone
Emotional	Quarrelsome
Strength	Aggression
Courage	Discord
Bold	Conservative
Confident	Conceited
Reflective	Disingenuous
Humanitarian	Interfering
Original	Unconventional
Innovative	Unorthodox
Able	Slapdash
Ambitious	Rebellious
Leader	Autocrat
Charismatic	Self-centred
Sexual vigour	Emotional insecurity
Affectionate	Vulnerable
Self-indulgence	Excess
Energy	Struggle
Expectation	Disappointment
Victory	Defeat

PERSONALITY

Nine was the crooked line of Pythagoras and his followers, and whilst they saw it as a number of intellect, its lack of symmetry symbolised for them the conflict between head and heart which governs the springs of all human action. Nine terminates the sequence of primary numbers, but in the flow of time it is at once the end and a beginning, having within it the seeds of rebirth and the potential for a fresh cycle of life. To the Greeks 10 was the number of infinity beyond 9. As infinity can never be reached, it and the numbers that follow it have no influence on character, except for the master numbers 11 and 22 – which in any case can be reduced to 2 and 4.

Nine has a unique property. When it is multiplied by any other primary number, including itself, the sum of the digits of the result is always 9. So $1 \times 9 = 9$, $2 \times 9 = 18$ and $1 + 8 = 9$, $3 \times 9 = 27$ and $2 + 7 = 9$, and so on. Thus, because it contains within it the qualities of every other number, Number 9 is the most powerful of them all. It stands for

energy, and people born under its influence are active and full of determination. They are rarely thinkers or planners in the way they approach
living. Rather, they launch into life with an excess of vim and vigour,
and if they are sometimes a little short on good sense, they can never be
accused of lacking courage. In fact courage is a keyword for Number 9s.
They are fighters who are always in the thick of any struggle, with a
wonderful never-say-die spirit which serves them very well at all times,
and helps them to get what they want out of life in the long term. They
will face problems and difficult periods like everyone else, but they,
more than any other numerological type, have the grit and determination to overcome most things. They have a tendency to regard compromise as a sign of weakness. This is no recipe for a peaceful, contented
existence, but even when they do occassionally turn the other cheek,
they do so unwillingly, often with a secret conviction that the risk of
defeat would have been preferable to making concessions.

Alongside this will to win is a strong independent streak which
tends to colour all their attitudes and actions. They desperately want to
be their own masters in all they do, following their instincts while ignor-
ing the advice of others. So they are something of a law unto themselves, and may not fit easily into conventional social stereotypes.

The main problem with such basically aggressive individuals is that
whilst their competitive spirit gives them an edge in those areas where
drive and a strong will are at a premium, it also involves them in strife
and conflict from which they may not emerge unscathed. At the same
time, unless the aggressive impulse is rigidly controlled and channelled,
it can lead to discord and confrontation in other parts of life where they
are not appropriate and may be positively harmful.

Number 9s are restless souls who are nearly always impulsive in
word and deed. If not actually conceited, they certainly have a good
opinion of themselves. For all their fighting qualities, they can be a bit
like babies who, with innocence on their side, regard themselves as the
most important thing in the world and who expect everyone else to
think so too. People of this vibration dislike interference intensely, and
even well-meant or valid criticism is likely to fall on deaf ears. They can
be rash, sometimes to the point of foolhardiness and, though they are
ready to jump in at the deep end at a moment's notice, they often lack
the patience to see out to the end what they have started, as they wear
themselves out in ceaseless mental or physical activity. On a purely
physical level they are prone to accident as a result of their tendency to
act before they think.

They have a temper too, and quarrels and scenes have a way of
following them everywhere they go. The fact is that they are very
emotional people who in the last analysis are ruled by their feelings and
gut reactions. They are often moved by instinct alone, with prejudices
conditioned by an emotional rather than an intellectual response to
people and events. Cheerful and optimistic, they seldom give way to
brooding or self-pity, but they do feel very deeply. So joys and sorrows
can move them to tears quite easily, and they pass quickly from the
heights of rapture to the depths of despair, sometimes over relative
trifles. Even abstractions like the sound of music or poetry have the

power to move them to a quite unusual degree. They are liable to fits of enthusiasm and these sudden bursts of energy may lead other people to see them as impractical, even slightly eccentric, if the result is that they act in an imprudent manner or in way that does not conform to normal modes of behaviour.

However, there is another aspect to the characters of typical Number 9 people. Though they are brave and relish a challenge, they may have a fear of the unknown and sometimes draw back from risks when the consequences cannot be calculated in advance. They are very much tied to their family background. Lacking the instinct for social mobility, the most talented of them may not rise as much in the world as they would have done if they had felt free to exploit their abilities to the full.

This innate conservatism stems from the other, reflective side to their personality which is often hidden by the sound and fury of their frequently contentious progress through everyday life. As we have seen, Pythagoras believed that 9 is one of the numbers which rules the mind. So even with their passionate natures, these people do sometimes stop to contemplate the deeper side of life. This may appear something of a contradiction, but for all their emotional, fiery response to many situations, they possess an intuitive grasp of what human beings are really like and how they interact in human affairs. The real contradiction is that Number 9s, though very aware of what makes other people tick, frequently lack the self-awareness needed to control the instinctive side of their own psyche. As they grow older, however, the restlessness and aggression which characterises the early years is usually moderated by a mellower, more contemplative view of life which in turn affects the way they behave.

Also, though they are always ready for a fight if what is at stake is important to them, they have a genuine love of their fellow human beings. This is no paradox either, for they are not naturally ruthless and their combative instinct is seldom devoid of feeling. With many Number 9s this sensitivity is translated into a genuine desire to help others. There are, for example, plenty of religious leaders and philanthropists in the Number 9 'Hall of Fame'. All Number 9s are sympathetic, tolerant and broad-minded, and they have a generous streak in their natures. This basic integrity is all the more a force for good because it is nearly always combined with a measure of practicality that enables them to achieve positive results.

In these circumstances it is not surprising that most people of this vibration are sociable and popular, although the caring side of their natures has a negative aspect too. In their desire to help, they can be nosy and domineering, and need to resist the temptation to interfere in what strictly speaking does not concern them.

On the whole, therefore, Number 9 is a fortunate number for those born under it, provided the more wayward and volatile tendencies are kept in check. Many Number 9 people who are basically unhappy with their lot owe their discontent to a failure to use the advantages conferred on them by their birth. In most cases the biggest single cause of this is the restlessness which leads them to flit from one goal to another, achieving little and exasperating, even alienating others as they go.

Provided the necessary restraint is exercised, people of this vibration are often enterprising and imaginative in their careers. They have the capacity to think on their feet and can usually see the quickest and most effective way to secure an aim or solve a problem. Pressure is meat and drink to them, so they are very useful individuals to have around in a crisis. The combination of courage and organisational flair which many of them possess can turn them into leaders who are both inspired and inspiring, with a real ability to motivate others.

Yet a lot of them who lack exceptional ability frequently experience difficulty in finding an outlet for the talents they have. Keen to experience what life has to offer, they like variety and change. As they are impatient, they may switch jobs several times, thus wasting the early years when the foundations of most successful careers are laid. They long for excitement and challenging situations. Denied this, they can rebel against a safe, orderly existence. Hence the possibility of their beginning to drift, which leads to frustration when they accomplish little in the long term. If, on the other hand, they choose and stick to careers which suit the other, more reflective side of their characters, they can still become frustrated by lack of action or excitement. For all these reasons the career road of many Number 9s can be a rocky one, with quite a few twists and turns, and no guarantee of ultimate professional fulfilment.

The type of job which suits them best will depend on whether the active or reflective tendency in their personalities is predominant. Those with creative ability often demonstrate great originality and are frequently found in the vanguard of new artistic movements. Their humanitatian instincts mean that they make good churchmen, doctors, dentists, hospital workers and counsellors in the caring professions. Alternatively, they may find that dangerous jobs have an irresistible lure. The armed forces appeal to many of them, and the more individualistic could gravitate towards unusual kinds of work which have a high element of risk.

Those Number 9s who settle into office work or other unadventurous jobs must successfully overcome the inherent defects of their character if they are to have real prospects of doing well. They need to control their impetuosity and must learn to think before they speak and act. Resenting criticism themselves, they are often over-critical of other people. If they habitually give way to this kind of conceit, they may end by being branded opinionated bores by both their peers and their superiors. They should accept that everyone has to start in a subordinate position, and resist the temptation to rock the boat when they do not get their own way or when promotion is slow in coming.

Successful Number 9s are good, if somewhat autocratic, bosses. They may be tough taskmasters, but they are never underhand and prefer to lead by example rather than by manipulation. They earn the respect of employees by their willingness to work just that bit harder than anyone else in the pursuit of team goals. Unsuccessful Number 9s are frustrated individuals who, for all their basic fighting qualities, may finally lose heart, letting their own work suffer in a way that in extreme cases can damage the efforts of their colleagues.

In their romantic dealings with the opposite sex, Number 9s, with their lively, outgoing temperament, can be devastatingly attractive – although they may not have the physical attributes that are usually considered sexually appealing. It is their inner strength, expressed in an animal magnetism, which draws others to them.

They have a lot of love to give and in turn crave plenty of affection themselves. In fact their desire for love is so powerful that they will go to all kinds of lengths to get it, even to the point of making fools of themselves over a member of the opposite sex they desire. Both men and women are suckers for the trappings of romance. The women expect to be bombarded with flowers and gifts as tokens of their suitor's love. Candlelit dinners in romantic settings can provide the heady atmosphere in which they can allow themselves to be seduced into a lasting commitment. As for the men, many of them plan their seductions with all the attention to detail of an eighteenth century rake and quickly become bored and disillusioned if the object of their attentions does not submit fairly quickly.

The problem for Number 9 men, both in courtship and marriage, is that they frequently confuse sex and real affection. So they are vulnerable in two ways. They often fall for a clever, scheming woman who knows what she has to do to ensnare a male who is so superficial in his attitude to love. Also, later on in marriage, they are completely at a loss if, through habit and routine, sexual passion cools from the peaks of physical ardour they expect. In this circumstance, for the immature Number 9, even repeated proofs of real affection and emotional loyalty will not entirely convince him that he has not been cheated in love.

However, Number 9 males set great store by family security and home comforts, so with the right woman they can slot easily into the pattern of conventional married life. Yet they remain sensualists, and could easily be susceptible to sexual temptation outside marriage, especially at difficult periods in their permanent relationship.

Number 9 females are strong and opinionated with a tendency, often unconscious, to try to 'manage' their sexual partner, especially if he is the compliant type. Physical sex is more important to them than for many women, and they may also exploit their own appetites in this respect to dominate a man who is responsive to what they have to offer sexually.

These women are, however, very far from being invulnerable in emotional relationships, and this is true even when, outwardly at least, they seem to be the dominant partner. Their sexual charms may not be as highly valued as they expect, and sometimes they find it difficult to express themselves emotionally in ways that are devoid of purely physical overtones. A woman of this number, despite her strength, may fight shy of confrontation with someone she loves. As a result dishonesty can creep into her relationship. She gets very angry when she feels let down or misunderstood by her lover, but is likely to bottle up her feelings inside. This perpetuates her emotional insecurity, and quite probably creates tension between herself and her partner, who may well be completely unaware of the reason for it.

Either in courtship or marriage, a woman of the ninth vibration has great difficulty in coping with any sort of rejection. If her man shows signs of unhappiness, she is apt to blame herself, perhaps quite unjustly. The consequence is that Number 9 women, the most overtly sexual of all women, begin to doubt the power of their own femininity. This is a serious blow to their self-esteem not just confined to the sexual sphere. It affects the whole of their conduct towards their lover, and sometimes the world in general.

On the whole, however, such problems are by no means certain to arise. Many marriages involving a Number 9 person of either sex work well, if only because Number 9s in general are sexual creatures who will never treat emotional problems with the indifference that often spells the end of love.

As wives, Number 9s are hardly ever submissive women happy to bow to their husband's every whim. At the very least they demand a partnership of equals, and usually get it. As husbands, the men can be inconsiderate when young, whatever the depth of their true feelings, and need a few knocks in life to teach them a little thoughtfulness. By and large, however, both sexes of this vibration make good companions who will try hard to fit in with their loved ones, at least on a superficial level. But more deeply, even when there is a great deal of love and external happiness, they may well over-analyse the inner workings of a relationship. It is not enough for them to know that it works. They need to know why it works, forever seeking reassurance and proofs of affection.

Also, because they are so emotionally charged, these people can be over-protective and sometimes jealous without real cause. Quarrels, both private and embarrassingly public, are very much part of the scene. Interference by in-laws, relatives or friends will tend to make things worse. A marriage of two Number 9s will be a very tempestuous relationship indeed.

Living with any Number 9 individual, therefore, is never easy. But nor is it ever likely to be dull or boring. Emotional excesses apart, Number 9s like variety in every aspect of domestic living and usually pursue an active social life in alliance with their partner, with many close friends and a wide circle of acquaintances.

Just as they are sensualists in matters of love, most Number 9s are extremely sensuous in other areas of life. They like physical warmth and comfort in the same way that they are at their most contented in the company of warm friends who enjoy, as they do, indulging all their physical appetites, as well as their taste for the luxuries of life. Given the wherewithal, typically the Number 9 person is to be found luxuriating in a bubbling jacuzzi before slipping between satin sheets to sleep off the effects of a sumptuous meal, washed down with large amounts of good wine. Even Number 9s who are not wealthy incline towards extravagance, and may experience regular difficulties when it comes to making the salary cheque last from one payday to the next. From the point of view of the maintenance of good health, excess in general, and particularly in any way that might affect the heart, must be guarded against.

People of this vibration are always a little larger than life. They may make the best of the assets conferred on them by birth, or they may fail in a material sense by dint of their inability to control the very traits which give them so much potential. But whether they are winners or losers on balance in life, they keep on trying. Only if completely disappointed and disillusioned will they find that their will to win leaves them in their hour of need. Extravagant in all things – emotionally, financially and in their goals and enthusiasms – their daily progress will be full of great joys and probably equally great sorrows. They feel so deeply and strive so hard that the smaller preoccupations of quieter, more restrained individuals pale into insignificance beside their victories and defeats – for they never do things by halves. They have big hearts to go with their big ideas. Even if in later life the physical engine which has worked so tirelessly in driving them on is vulnerable, as long as they have breath in their bodies they will go on struggling to the end. Only if the years have treated them very harshly will they compromise and settle for anything less than total commitment to the battle of life.

NUMBER 9 CHILDREN

Anyone reading the above portrait of the typical adult 9 could be forgiven for thinking that very young children of this vibration are bound to be egocentric little monsters! They will demand more attention than most children and they are not above a tantrum if they do not get their own way, but there is no reason why these youngsters should degenerate into spoiled brats from an early age. The parent who makes it clear who is the boss from the beginning and who restrains their infant's excesses in an understanding way will be rewarded by a child with many good and endearing qualities.

Happy, optimistic, with a natural empathy for all sorts of young people their own age, Number 9 children will never hide their light under a bushel. Conceited and boisterous they may be, but with the right guidance they can be turned into responsible human beings at least as early as any other personality type.

When they go to school, tears of anger or frustration may surface from time to time, but this shows that they care. They give 100% all the time, so they may succeed academically, possibly against the odds. Even if they fall some way short in this respect, there will be plenty of other skills or talents that they can throw themselves heart and soul into developing.

If they want to leave home sooner rather than later, they should not be opposed. They are much more likely to swim than sink in the grown-up world, and they certainly need to complete their education in the university of life before tackling seriously the long term hopes and expectations before them.

COLOUR

In the psychology of the colours brown is representative of all things physical in opposition to more spiritual preoccupations. So brown will satisfy the Number 9 individual's need for physical comfort and security. It will also reinforce the satisfaction they get from the physical presence of congenial company by providing an ambience which in their own minds is receptive to it. Even in a hostile setting this colour will always provide the Number 9 person with a measure of comfort.

Brown is a blend of orange and black and allows Number 9s to express the energy and cheerfulness of their personalities, while moderating the tendency to revolt in the face of a too conventional or restricting environment.

Red, however, should be avoided as far as possible. It is the colour of passion or anger, and will only reinforce the volatility which, if carried to excess, may damage people of this vibration.

FAMOUS NUMBER 9 PEOPLE

☆ **Monarchs** ☆
★ Frederick the Great of Prussia, King Juan Carlos of Spain ★
☆ **Modern British Royalty** ☆
★ Prince Michael of Kent ★
☆ **Politicians** ☆
★ Neville Chamberlain, David Lloyd George, Nelson Mandela, ★
Helmut Schmidt
☆ **Soldier/politician** ☆
★ General Franco ★
☆ **Soldiers** ☆
★ Glubb Pasha, Erwin Rommel ★
☆ **Religious Leaders** ☆
★ Mahatma Gandhi, Billy Graham ★
☆ **Philanthropists** ☆
★ Albert Schweitzer, William Wilberforce ★
☆ **Scientists** ☆
★ Carl Jung, Joseph Lister ★
☆ **Writers** ☆
★ Arnold Bennett, Barbara Cartland, Joseph Conrad, ★
Frederick Forsyth, Robert Graves, Georgette Heyer, Hammond
Innes, Desmond Morris, Edna O'Brien, John Osborne
☆ **Artists** ☆
★ David Hockney, Henry Moore, Ben Nicholson, Auguste Rodin ★
☆ **Musicians** ☆
★ Glen Miller, Cole Porter ★
☆ **Singers** ☆
★ Lena Horne, Kiri Te Kanawa, Elvis Presley, Joan Sutherland ★
☆ **Actors and actresses** ☆
★ Brigitte Bardot, Peter Barkworth, Alan Bates, Ian Carmichael, ★
Michael Crawford, Bette Davis, Harrison Ford, Liza Goddard,
Dustin Hoffman, Anthony Hopkins, Felicity Kendall,
Shirley MacLaine, Merlina Mercouri, Ethel Merman,
Paul Schofield

☆ **Media personalities** ☆
★ Eamonn Andrews, Rowan Atkinson, Joan Bakewell, ★
Jasper Carrott, Sam Goldwyn,Barry Humphries, Jonathan Miller,
Michael Palin

☆ **Sportsmen and women** ☆
★ Peter Beardsley, Will Carling, David Gower, Jimmy Greaves, ★
Allan Lamb, Jack Nicklaus, Viv Richards, Mark Spitz

NUMBER 11

When the birth number reduces to 11 before the final 2 in the manner illustrated in Chapter 2, it could be that the individual in question falls into a special category outside the main patterns of personality encompassed in the primary numbers 1 to 9.

Number 11 is a master number and those Number 2s who are also Number 11s can live on a more elevated spiritual plane than other people. This may not necessarily be the case, but genuine Number 11s have the potential to spread illumination in the world through special, intuitive powers exercised in either word or deed. They are therefore capable of great achievement, though few of them will ever realise anything like the limits of this unusual capacity. Also, true Number 11s who have gone some way towards developing their inspirational powers may suffer from an inner conflict. This pulls them in different directions in their external life as they fight to resolve the contradictions of a dual personality, one ordinary and unexceptional, the other fundamentally the same but infused with a rare gift. Even if the development falls very far short of final completion, once begun it results in Number 11s having a great deal to offer others, though those closest to them may find them difficult to live with because of their inner struggle.

Number 11s are above all idealists. They are ready to fight for the principles they believe to be right and may have a genuine love of their fellow human beings. So if they can convert their special, initially latent powers into real and positive action, they may devote their lives to helping others. This is not to say that they will necessarily become philanthropists in the true sense, but they are invariably prepared to put their special gift to the service of some cause higher than their own material interest, and may even neglect the needs of their loved ones or immediate dependents in pursuit of it. In addition, they will probably display many of the characteristic failings of the typical idealist, especially when their potential lies dormant within them or when they cannot find a proper channel for it. So they can be dreamy and impractical, and may end by achieving nothing at all. This can cause frustration and unhappiness – which in an extreme form manifests itself in a feeling of having wasted their lives.

A good historical example of a Number 11 who did realise his potential to the fullest extent is the Duke of Wellington. Born on 1st May, 1769, the 'Iron Duke' was a truly remarkable individual. Victor of Waterloo and later Prime Minister of his country, he became a national hero and a legend in his own lifetime. He was first and foremost a patriot who served his nation exceptionally in its hour of greatest need, but he was also a High Tory idealist, not to say bigot. His stubborn opposition to the reform of the franchise in accordance with his Tory principles led to the fall of his government and the end of his own political career. Yet for all his military genius and lofty patriotism, there was no ordinary philanthropy in him. He had the reputation of being a very cold fish indeed, and described the men he commanded as 'the mere scum of the earth'. Thus the interests of the soldiers who made his victories possible and any affection an ordinary man might have felt for them were subordinated to the infinitely greater cause of saving England from Napoleon.

Of course not every Number 11 will scale the heights achieved by a Wellington. They may get to the top in their chosen field, but they are not all leaders. They are sometimes prone to stress and worry if their special power is not fully in tune with the external world and their place in it. But whatever their wordly attainments, they generally display the enthusiasm and vigour found in many persons born under Number 9, as well as the sensitivity of a Number 2 with none of the failings typical of that number. If developed, the special power of Number 11s manifests itself in an ability to inspire. This may be as an individual of some consequence exercising power and influence over other people, or as a sympathetic person who earns respect and admiration in a quiet way among his or her peers. Though they are nearly always listened to and may be able to affect how others behave, they do not invariably attract love or affection because of it. They are frequently cool and undemonstrative – private people with an air of detachment who can be difficult to get to know well. Once the ice is broken, however, they make true and loyal friends with those people for whom they feel a particular empathy.

Nearly all Number 11s live on a knife edge between positive and negative, spiritual and material, and even between good and evil. The powerful ones need to be wary of using their special gift for selfish ends at the expense of ordinary human compassion, whereas the weak ones, lacking firmness and consistency, are apt to drift in life. The latter must take a determined hold of their own lives, thereby freeing themselves from the influence of others stronger than themselves, and becoming much less vulnerable to the vicissitudes of chance. In a few cases where the balance between right and wrong is distorted towards moral weakness, these people can be very dangerous individuals with a malevolent tendency that can do great harm.

Most people with this special vibration are a power for good in the world. They may fulfil the extraordinary mission made possible by their birth, thereby giving far more than they receive during their life. Alternatively, they may never realise the potential of their special station, suffering varying degrees of frustration because of it. Either way, they are privileged people who are found only rarely in the range of human types.

NUMBER 22

Number 4s who are also Number 22s have the capacity to become very rare individuals. This is because Number 22 is potentially the number of the truly exceptional human being. When the power of this vibration is fully developed, those who come under its influence are likely to combine all or most of the best qualities found in the personalities of every other numerological type. It bestows the intelligence of Number 1, the sensitivity and affability of Number 2, the vivacity of Number 3, the capacity for hard work of Number 4, the enterprise of Number 5, the charisma of Number 6, the vision of Number 7, the determination of Number 8, the courage of Number 9 and the idealism of Number 11.

It should be no surprise, therefore, that the perfect balance and limitless potential implied in this master number is hardly ever found in any large sample of Number 4s who also possess the Number 22 vibration. So a Number 4 who is also a Number 22 may have none of the attributes of the latter. Even the Number 4/22 person with the inborn gift that might conceivably enable them to exist on the higher plane is not very likely to make the necessary conversion in the fullest sense. In fact the reverse is often the case. Precisely because the possibilities for ultimate achievement are so great, Number 4s who are also Number 22s have the greatest capacity of all for wasting the potential of their birth.

People with some of the qualities of Number 22 are apt to be workaholics who are quick-witted and far-sighted, and who may do very well in life. They are nearly always sincere, rather romantic individuals who are much sought after as good company and valued friends. However, even if only half aware of their unusual gifts, they run a grave risk of being complacent in important areas of life. They often feel that there is nothing the world or other people can teach them once they have applied themselves and mastered a field of endeavour. Also, they sometimes fail to see that the material plane is only one aspect of human attainment, and they can fall victim to the moral dangers of self-seeking and acquisitiveness. Arrogance is also a weakness from which many of them are not immune.

As for those Number 22s who fail entirely to bring out the hidden force within them, they may, like Number 11s, turn out to be impractical dreamers who lose themselves in empty longing, whilst failing to make the necessary effort to accomplish anything of value at all. Some of them may retreat from the world entirely in one way or another. They often strike other people as persons with great potential who for some unaccountable reason have wasted their talents. Individual cases vary, but in the main the root cause of their disappointment and eventual rejection of any attempt to follow their potential destiny stems from their failure to come to terms with the restless, nervous tension that accompanies their latent powers. Instead of a driving force, it is a burden to them. Struggling with inner forces they do not comprehend, they are completely unable to harmonise them with the external world, and as a result become lost, even rather pathetic souls adrift on the ocean of life.

But Number 22s who can function as human beings within the highly charged field of their unique vibration, and who are able to draw on it for positive action, are among the true luminaries in the firmament of human achievement. Her Majesty Queen Elizabeth the Queen Mother and Margaret Thatcher, though two very different sorts of people, have been excellent examples of the best of the Number 4/22 vibration. Whatever your political affiliations or your view of royalty, they have led outstanding lives which demonstrate what is possible when the potential of this master number is realised.

YOUR DAILY LIFEGUIDE

INTRODUCTION

You can use the analysis in Chapter 2 to assess, with a reasonable degree of accuracy, the personalities of both yourself and other people. But you must bear in mind that the lives of all of us are in a state of constant flux. A numerological reading of character alone does not enable us to chart the course of our daily lives according to the vibration of numbers.

However, you can extend the basic ideas of numerology to build up a picture of life trends from day to day. The way this is done is to relate personality – as the source of human action – to the vibrations produced by the movement of time. Just as individuals have life numbers, dates in the year are also governed by a numerical vibration. For instance the vibration for 2 May 1994 is calculated as 2/5/1994; **2**, **5**,1 + 9 + 9 + 4 = **23**; 2 + 5 + 23 = **30** and 3 + 0 = **3**. Days of the week also are subject to vibrations which favour some aspects of life and which may have a less beneficial or even adverse effect on others. Also, two numbers may be neutral in relation to each other, some numbers harmonise, whereas other combinations strike a discordant note.

You will have already worked out your birth number. Now work out the date number for today's date and find the page in this Lifeguide that gives both these numbers. You will find a specific reading for the day of the week on which the date falls. As a result you can gain insights into some of the problems that currently confront you, and even some guidance on how best to deal with them.

Use this worksheet to find the date number each time you consult the Lifeguide.

Date of consultation:	......**/**......**/**......
Stage 1:	......**+**......**=**......;......**+**......**=**......
	......**+**......**+**......**+**......**=**......
Stage 2:	......**+**......**+**......**=**......
Stage 3:	......**+**......**=**......
	and if needed,......**+**......**=**......
Date number:	

BIRTH NUMBER 1 – DATE NUMBER 1

SUNDAY

The present phase is one where you are prepared to move heaven and earth to carry everyone with you. You won't always be right, but the personal cost of a few minor errors should be more than compensated for by the benefits of a highly positive approach.

MONDAY

Financial concerns have a high profile at the moment. Remember, money is a good servant, but a bad master.

TUESDAY

You may have to do what your partner wants, even if you are not entirely in agreement. However there is no reason why you shouldn't enjoy yourself. In fact you could be in for a pleasant surprise!

WEDNESDAY

You have so many good ideas at this time that you may be literally spoilt for choice. Varying degrees of risk will be involved, so weigh the odds very carefully in relation to chances.

THURSDAY

At home others will look for a lead, but you may be inclined to opt out this once. Make the effort, however, and you should be rewarded with a happy outcome for everyone, including yourself.

FRIDAY

This could be a good day for romance or social life, but don't spoil it by thinking only of yourself. There is absolutely nothing wrong with standing on your own two feet. However your obsession with independence can be very off-putting to others, even those who care most about you.

SATURDAY

You are exceptionally busy, but have you stopped to consider that the resulting irregularities in your lifestyle are not making your home life any easier for yourself or the rest of the family?

BIRTH NUMBER 1 – DATE NUMBER 2

SUNDAY

The stresses and strains of the current period in your life may seem unavoidable, but are you really so indispensable in every department? Let others do some of the worrying for a change. It just isn't necessary for you to have a finger in every single pie.

MONDAY

A good friend may give you some sound advice, but the intuition of a loved one could prove more accurate in predicting how things will actually turn out.

TUESDAY

You may be romantically inclined at the moment. However it might be that your idyllic view of love isn't shared by someone much more down-to-earth. Try to see their point of view but, if you can't meet on the same level, it may be best to cut your losses and move on.

WEDNESDAY

The desire to rule the roost is natural to you, though this is not always to your advantage. Try to recognise those situations where a low profile is best for your personal cause. Then make a conscious effort to give your ego a well-earned rest.

THURSDAY

Any temptation to ignore an unpleasant truth at this time may cause you to do a disservice to others as well as yourself.

FRIDAY

What you want doesn't necessarily correspond to the needs or desires of other people, at home just as much as anywhere else. Riding roughshod won't help, and even compromise might not prove altogether satisfactory. It may go against the grain, but a climbdown, adroitly managed to save your pride, could be the best thing for all concerned.

SATURDAY

Stale relationships are probably due for a shake-up. Only you can decide how much of the past you wish to endure, but events could develop a momentum of their own, independent of your wishes.

BIRTH NUMBER 1 – DATE NUMBER 3

SUNDAY

The current phase is one where your personal obsessions tend to override the dictates of moderation and good sense. Be more flexible.

MONDAY

Financial uncertainties may be paralysing domestic plans. Be content to wait until the picture becomes clearer.

TUESDAY

Your inclination not to afford other people the respect they deserve is acting as a brake on your progress. On the other hand give them a bit more credit than they are, strictly speaking, due and you will be amazed what doors open to you.

WEDNESDAY

Some of your old demons reappear to disturb home life. You won't be popular unless you can see the other point of view.

THURSDAY

You seem quick to take offence, a sure sign that you are driving yourself too hard. However indispensable you regard yourself, there must be ways of taking things a little easier without impairing your overall efficiency.

FRIDAY

Your skill in difficult situations is a major asset. Do not become conceited because of it. Modesty becomes you and heightens your capacity to manage people and events.

SATURDAY

A fresh romantic wind may be about to blow through your life, but beware of being seduced by sexual style. Substance is what counts in the end.

BIRTH NUMBER 1 – DATE NUMBER 4

SUNDAY

Because a bit of bluster has got you out of difficulties in the past, you have a tendency to think that a high-handed manner will always achieve the desired result. Not everyone can be pushed around, however, so think twice before trying to solve a current problem by throwing your weight about.

MONDAY

Keep your options open today. The right course to adopt may not be revealed until the very last minute.

TUESDAY

If it isn't possible to change your surroundings in any significant way, you should look for ways and means of grafting an extra dimension onto your current way of life. Not easy of course, but stagnation eats away at your soul.

WEDNESDAY

Some people seem intent on stealing a march over you. You might just have to accept that for the time being at least there isn't much you can do about it. Your time will come.

THURSDAY

You want sympathy and understanding from someone, but you still think you are entitled to be offhand or even bad-tempered when it suits you. What is needed is a change of heart by you. Begin by apologising.

FRIDAY

You possess the gift of originality, but you remain convinced the world you inhabit offers too little scope to develop it. Your defeatism does you no credit. In fact there is an opportunity round every corner.

SATURDAY

Try to be patient if you encounter resistance to what you think is a quite sensible proposal. In reality you find the quirkier aspects of your family life rather appealing. A heavy hand or a sharp tongue could easily spoil the idiosyncratic charm.

BIRTH NUMBER 1 – DATE NUMBER 5

SUNDAY

You do seem to be slightly at odds with the rest of the world at present. This probably reflects an inner conflict over what you are and what you would like to be. Unravelling the knot of tension won't be easy, but try not to be so rigid in your approach to life. Bend and others will bend with you.

MONDAY

Treat any sales pitch in your direction with extreme caution. Some people are just too glib to be taken seriously. Gossips are also likely to be seeking their own ends.

TUESDAY

If the course of true love isn't running smoothly, try to control your need to dominate. More give and less take is the prescription for a happier relationship.

WEDNESDAY

Keeping up with the Joneses may be proving expensive. Examine your financial priorities.

THURSDAY

The dominant mood of the day may be one of suspicion. However if you see a challenge to your power or authority at every turn, you could be misreading the situation.

FRIDAY

Those with relatives abroad may soon receive news of an unexpected development. Even a letter or postcard from nearer home may cause a ripple of surprise.

SATURDAY

Don't let success go to your head if you have made a significant advance in your career lately. Your high opinion of yourself may well be justified, but keep it to yourself over the coming weeks.

BIRTH NUMBER 1 – DATE NUMBER 6

SUNDAY

Under this configuration of numbers you don't have your usual reserves of energy. Also, you may lack concentration and have a tendency to be forgetful. Have you been wasting your emotions on trifles? You are inclined to introspection anyway, but the cumulative effect of too much soul-searching can be very damaging.

MONDAY

Any aches and pains can be dispelled by some not too vigorous exercise. Try working out to music or join an aerobics class. Physical exertion may then become a pleasure. You will feel so much better for making the effort.

TUESDAY

Perhaps because you attach more importance to ideas than things or even people, your memory could have been playing some funny tricks in routine areas. Don't run away with the idea that influential people do not notice when you aren't quite on the ball. You will be judged by what others see and hear.

WEDNESDAY

Time is running out if you have been putting off a decision over something to do with home maintenance.

THURSDAY

Your abilities are considerable, but do not overrate them. Others are talented too, and you don't have a monopoly of being the best.

FRIDAY

You might be surprised if you knew what other people really thought of you. The time will almost certainly come when you find out. In the meanwhile, ask yourself whether their views are likely to be favourable or otherwise.

SATURDAY

Stop trying to twist people round your little finger. Few of them are as weak or gullible as you sometimes imagine. Sooner or later some of those clever little ploys of yours could backfire in a big way.

BIRTH NUMBER 1 – DATE NUMBER 7

SUNDAY

Don't compromise your romantic ideals. If you allow yourself to be rushed into things against your better judgement, you may have cause to repent. Remember, everything comes to he (or she) who waits.

MONDAY

You are a very capable sort of person, but the touching faith of others in your ability to cope with almost any situation puts a lot of extra pressure on you. Also, it may be that your own expectations are sometimes too high. Don't sell yourself short, but a more moderate set of ambitions would certainly lessen the double strain you often feel.

TUESDAY

Where a conflict between career and home interests is concerned, you and you alone can decide which way to jump, for only you know what your real priorities are. A compromise, unfortunately, may be difficult to achieve.

WEDNESDAY

Today could be full of conflict through no fault of your own, but don't dig your heels in if you find yourself faced with opposition you instinctively know is too strong to overcome.

THURSDAY

The centre of the stage attracts you, but you should be certain of your ability to give a good performance once there. Are you?

FRIDAY

Minor problems need to be tackled if harmony is to be maintained. Sometimes it can seem that domestic trifles claim an excessive amount of your time but, by neglecting your obligations in this respect, you will make a rod for your own back.

SATURDAY

You may have mixed feelings over someone else's attitude, but resist the temptation to interfere. Follow Voltaire's famous dictum and 'cultivate your garden', leaving others to be responsible for their own affairs.

BIRTH NUMBER 1 – DATE NUMBER 8

SUNDAY

A new phase in your life is imminent. The best of the old may be the soundest foundation for the new, and be wary of taking refuge in false hopes.

MONDAY

If a power struggle develops, you should remember that true strength implies gentleness. Minimum necessary force should be your guiding principle, whatever the nature of the conflict.

TUESDAY

Don't expect to make a name for yourself overnight. Your reputation will be enhanced by commitment and perseverance long term, not a single flash of brilliance. Shooting stars burn out very quickly.

WEDNESDAY

If you are counting the days to a holiday, it could be worthwhile making sure that all matters of detail have been scrupulously attended to.

THURSDAY

Strange as it may seem, you are on the point of a breakthrough. However, you will need to recognise the exact moment when to force the pace.

FRIDAY

Your recent tendency to be insensitive, even ruthless, could have unfortunate consequences. What you think of as a sign of your own inner strength may be viewed very differently in other quarters.

SATURDAY

You are too easily distracted by frivolities. Enjoy yourself by all means, but don't forget your responsibilities.

BIRTH NUMBER 1 – DATE NUMBER 9

SUNDAY

Some people may be in the mood to reminisce. Join in. Shared memories bring everyone together in a congenial way.

MONDAY

If it transpires that a chapter in your life is really coming to a close, don't worry unduly about how things are going to turn out. You have a lot of style, and it should take you where you want to go. But don't overplay your hand in unfamiliar situations.

TUESDAY

People have as much right to their views and convictions as you have to your own. A closed mind will get you nowhere.

WEDNESDAY

All things pass. Therefore excessive exultation or depression are equally misplaced in the scheme of things. Good follows bad, and bad follows good.

THURSDAY

Emotions can't be turned on and off like a tap. Remember this if you embark on a relationship where total commitment may eventually be required of you.

FRIDAY

Good luck is a precious commodity. If some of it comes your way, capitalise on it for all it is worth.

SATURDAY

Those in long-term relationships should accept the fact that someone usually has to take the lead. But it is harmful for one person to make all the decisions all the time.

BIRTH NUMBER 2 – DATE NUMBER 1

SUNDAY

There is really no reason to settle for second best if, as you suspect, one final push can overcome major obstacles to your happiness. Take the bull by the horns.

MONDAY

In the struggle to get ahead, you usually prefer to play a waiting game, but at the moment you do seem determined to get really stuck in. Remember, however, that even if you win a battle, you don't necessarily win the war.

TUESDAY

An inexpensive purchase may bring happiness out of all proportion to its cost. Alert collectors may make a find.

WEDNESDAY

Share any good fortune with friends or relatives. The pleasure you get will be increased as a result.

THURSDAY

You're a lot more resourceful than perhaps you realise. So when people are willing to depend on you, take this for the compliment it is, and accept the credit that's due. If this means stepping into the limelight for a change, then why not? A boost to your ego will do no harm at all.

FRIDAY

You are inclined to take risks just now. Gamble for love, not money.

SATURDAY

The genuine feeling you have for your fellow human beings will always be the source of your greatest personal fulfilment. Even apparently little things will provide a large measure of satisfaction. Be true to yourself, and let others chase the pot of gold at the end of the rainbow.

BIRTH NUMBER 2 – DATE NUMBER 2

SUNDAY
Family and friends can't understand your attitude to a matter which has a bearing on everyone's life. If you are acting out of character, it may be right to reconsider your motives.

MONDAY
Envy and jealousy may come to the surface if other people seem to be outstripping you in important areas. Forget about others and concentrate on what you can do to help yourself.

TUESDAY
Authority figures seem unprepared to allow you much room for manoeuvre, so any thought of making progress with large-scale plans may have to be shelved. Don't get angry. Consolidate your position by careful attention to detail. Recognition will come sooner or later.

WEDNESDAY
You will never be entirely free of your habitual tendency to fret over trivialities, but you won't get rattled so easily if you make a deliberate attempt to see to the heart of matters. The really important things in any single life are surprisingly few.

THURSDAY
If you are honest with yourself, you will probably admit you are apt to blame others when things go awry. Is it possible that, however wronged you may feel, on this occasion a problem is largely of your own making?

FRIDAY
Age and experience bring strength of a sort, but it will always be brittle as long as your will to win is weak. If only you weren't so pessimistic, the daily struggle wouldn't seem quite so arduous.

SATURDAY
Your penchant for crying wolf where cash is concerned sometimes causes resentment among others who suspect that in reality things aren't quite so bad as you make out. Pay up with a smile.

BIRTH NUMBER 2 - DATE NUMBER 3

SUNDAY
If you have artistic leanings, you may not get much sympathy from more mundane types. Imagination needs the right milieu in which to flourish, and you might have to widen your circle of acquaintances before you can spread your creative wings.

MONDAY
You would probably admit you're not a natural leader, but you could find yourself with a pivotal role in a difficult situation. Don't be alarmed. Keep your head and everything will be fine.

TUESDAY
The superficial charm of someone in your life hides a ruthless streak. If you haven't identified the person in question by now, it's time you psychoanalysed a few of the people in your immediate circle.

WEDNESDAY
Cash may be in short supply. So if you are intent on making a necessary purchase, don't let yourself be fobbed off with second best. However urgent things seem, give yourself time to buy what you really want and need.

THURSDAY
You must say what you think for a change. Otherwise others will see you as a nonentity with no opinions of your own.

FRIDAY
In any close relationship it's not unusual for one party to feel more deeply than the other. If you are the less sensitive one, a false move by you could widen any existing gap. If your feelings are the more vulnerable, remember that taking the rough with the smooth is a part of life.

SATURDAY
Forget worries about the future and concentrate on the here and now. There's a lot of fun to be had if you can be carefree even for a short while.

BIRTH NUMBER 2 – DATE NUMBER 4

SUNDAY

You have been on something of an emotional rollercoaster lately, with highs and lows following one another in quick succession. Before you reach for the tranquillisers, stop to consider what is causing the swings in mood. The broader pattern of your life is much more important than minor twists of fate.

MONDAY

There's a world of difference between being assertive and being aggressive. Without going to extremes, you should certainly challenge anyone who tries to thwart your progress by unfair means.

TUESDAY

If you're feeling off-colour, the cause could be due to your state of mind. Worry or strain is much more likely to be the culprit than a mystery ailment.

WEDNESDAY

Women of this number should realise that most men want a wife and mistress as a partner, not a mother or a child. Number 2 men mustn't mistake a show of friendship for an erotic signal.

THURSDAY

A period of domestic happiness is in the offing. Only an excess of pessimism about the long-term future can spoil things. Don't let it.

FRIDAY

The competitive edge is razor sharp at work. If you can't bring yourself to see your friends as possible enemies, then you should at least look upon your enemies as potential friends.

SATURDAY

Curb your desire to spend. Today is important, but so is tomorrow.

BIRTH NUMBER 2 – DATE NUMBER 5

SUNDAY

A foreign influence may be about to play a part in your life, but only if you are receptive to impulses alien to your usual way of looking at the world.

MONDAY

It's possible your feelings of dissatisfaction are due to a series of niggles for which you have only yourself to blame. Learn from the past and turn over a new leaf. A repetition of previous errors could have far more serious consequences next time around.

TUESDAY

Single people looking for a safe haven in love could be knocking at the wrong door. A much more passionate and adventurous approach is needed for romantic success.

WEDNESDAY

If you're discontented in your career, you have a real problem. The only lasting solution is a radical one, but if you don't feel ready for a change, or the opportunity for it is just not there, you will have to take yourself in hand and make the best of things, at least for the time being.

THURSDAY

Petty prejudices could damage your relations with others. Try to be more objective in your dealings with people.

FRIDAY

Outwardly you appear indifferent to everyone and everything. This is not the real you, and in the long run self-protection of this kind could prove as damaging to you as it is hurtful to others.

SATURDAY

Several in the family circle may have had more than their fair share of disappointments recently, but they have to realise that resources just won't run to the satisfaction of every whim. If you're not the main provider, try to understand the point of view of the person who is.

BIRTH NUMBER 2 – DATE NUMBER 6

SUNDAY

If you can face domestic difficulties with a sunny disposition, you will certainly find light at the end of the tunnel.

MONDAY

Too many of your attitudes are outmoded. You need to move with the times, so be more receptive to new ideas.

TUESDAY

There's trouble in the air. If you really don't know what's up, look for a deeper meaning in apparently casual and inconsequential remarks.

WEDNESDAY

Loved ones, children and friends are enriching your life. You must find ways to show that you appreciate it.

THURSDAY

If past ties are dragging you down, you should ask yourself why you are unable to make a clean break. Could it be that you have nothing really substantial or worthwhile to put in their place?

FRIDAY

You are learning to like yourself better. The more this process continues, the more others will respond to you. However, never try to be something you're not.

SATURDAY

You often worry about the future, but if you discuss your hopes with other members of the family, you may well find that their conception of what tomorrow should bring doesn't coincide with your own in several important respects.

BIRTH NUMBER 2 – DATE NUMBER 7

SUNDAY

Breaking promises to others isn't your style, but what about the promises you have made to yourself? Often you seem unwilling to 'go the last mile' to achieve self-fulfilment. You should definitely ask yourself why.

MONDAY

Don't meet an obstacle head on. Go round it. Your intelligence will enable you to get the timing right.

TUESDAY

Promotions are in the offing, but you are unsure of your prospects. Don't get left behind. You're much more highly thought of than perhaps you realise.

WEDNESDAY

You may be a stickler with others if a principle is at stake, especially when your own interests are affected. But however much you tell yourself the end justifies the means, are your own methods always above reproach?

THURSDAY

Home is all of a sudden a hive of activity. Keep the pot boiling for as long as possible. Things have been too dull for too long.

FRIDAY

This is an excellent day for renewing contacts, either on the business or social front. Don't let feelings of diffidence hold you back. Just getting in touch with people who have similar interests to your own could be mutually advantageous.

SATURDAY

It's possible that the very opposite of what you expect to happen will actually occur. Therefore formulate an alternative plan of action in good time.

BIRTH NUMBER 2 – DATE NUMBER 8

SUNDAY

Outside influences are having an adverse influence on the happy home. Are you getting your priorities right?

MONDAY

You could get lucky if you seize an opportunity without procrastinating. Hesitate and all may be lost. It's not always obvious when fate is beckoning, so you will need all your wits about you in order not to miss out.

TUESDAY

Complications in your emotional life won't be helped by your tendency to take the line of least resistance. Whether you like it or not, firmness will be needed to stop any further deterioration.

WEDNESDAY

You may be short of the facts which seem necessary to make progress. Yet those in authority and also your peers might be reluctant to help. Is there a mystery to be solved? At any rate, if no one will take you into their confidence, the obvious question is 'Why?'

THURSDAY

If the relative calm of tender affection without sexual or emotional fireworks is what turns you on most, you could have to wait quite a while before attaining your heart's desire.

FRIDAY

You may have stumbled recently, without actually falling. Either way, you should consider what went wrong and make sure you don't do the same again.

SATURDAY

The solution to a current difficulty depends on you and you alone. Others are being reasonable. Are you?

BIRTH NUMBER 2 – DATE NUMBER 9

SUNDAY

Decisions taken now may have consequences far beyond the immediate horizon, so it's vital to listen to everyone's point of view. However, those who are most strident won't necessarily be right.

MONDAY

There's definitely a change in the air, but you are having a hard time in seeing which way the wind blows. This could be because of a chaotic situation in some aspect of your life. A clear head and steady nerves will enable you to bring the ship back on course.

TUESDAY

Time spent on reconnaissance is seldom wasted. Therefore, examine all the angles before finally committing yourself. The sincerity of potential associates should be checked out too.

WEDNESDAY

If not exactly one of nature's subordinates, nevertheless you have always worked well under supervision. Resist any temptation to go out on a limb. Your progress will be maintained if you stick to tried and trusted ways.

THURSDAY

Anyone who is avoiding you no doubt has their reasons. Have you really considered what they might be?

FRIDAY

Devotion to duty is required to get you through a difficult patch. Constancy now will pay a dividend later on.

SATURDAY

What you need most today is time to think. Make sure you get it, and don't let anyone distract you, even at the risk of giving minor offence.

BIRTH NUMBER 3 – DATE NUMBER 1

SUNDAY

If you decide to extricate yourself from a close alliance, do it gradually without attracting too much attention. A clean break is often best, but not on this occasion.

MONDAY

Careful planning now should pay off later on. It's not that you haven't thought about the future, you almost certainly have, but it's time to convert vague ideas into definite objectives. Drifting along from day to day is comfortable and undemanding, but it doesn't get you very far.

TUESDAY

If you are contemplating an expensive purchase, it's worth remembering that what is new today is often discarded tomorrow.

WEDNESDAY

Hope for the best and prepare for the worst is sound advice if some people's predictions of doom and gloom are about to be tested.

THURSDAY

Your current evasions could easily earn you a reputation as an unprincipled schemer. Only a change of stance will convince others that you mean what you say.

FRIDAY

Science in one of its many applications may provide the solution to a long-standing problem. Get expert advice if you're unsure.

SATURDAY

You need space and a sense of freedom. Outdoor pursuits are definitely favoured at the moment.

BIRTH NUMBER 3 – DATE NUMBER 2

SUNDAY

There's probably no real cause for concern on the health front, but there may be room for improvement in the way you treat yourself. Diet and exercise are obvious starting points.

MONDAY

Time and tide wait for no man. Delay now could permanently damage your current ambitions.

TUESDAY

You're a rebel without a cause at the moment. Only a real sense of purpose and the determination to impose it on your life and actions will bring a change of luck.

WEDNESDAY

Avoid going on a spending spree just now. There may be things you want and things you think you must have, but financial prudence is called for. Above all, don't be 'penny wise, pound foolish' just because you are feeling a bit low.

THURSDAY

You have to admit that you can be gullible at times, and in the past you've often been a soft touch, either emotionally or financially. Don't be afraid to say 'No' to unreasonable demands. You can make concessions from a position of strength if they seem justified later on.

FRIDAY

You have a tendency to build castles in the air. Your present mood of wild optimism could be so misplaced that it's positively dangerous.

SATURDAY

Several alternatives hold a superficial attraction. Stick to what you know, whatever the temptations in other directions.

BIRTH NUMBER 3 – DATE NUMBER 3

SUNDAY

It's a moot point whether every cloud has a silver lining. So if a separation is in the air, prepare yourself for a difficult period of readjustment.

MONDAY

Adverse comment about your professional commitment will obviously hurt. If you have been taking a bit of a free ride lately, now is the time to put matters right.

TUESDAY

Home life may seem claustrophobic at the moment, but true freedom is the freedom to choose. However oppressive domestic concerns appear, would you really choose a rootless life without security or comfort?

WEDNESDAY

Apathy, negligence or frivolity may cause you to act stupidly at a key moment. You have been warned.

THURSDAY

Ignore gossip throughout the day. It might well be malicious in intent, and your best course is to give a wide berth to controversy of any kind.

FRIDAY

Good fortune may be on the way, and you can increase the odds in your favour if you work harder.

SATURDAY

Your herd instinct is highly developed and you will never be short of a friend in your hour of need. But there are times when the majority opinion isn't necessarily right, at least in so far as your own interests are concerned. Sometimes you have to make up your mind to plough a lone furrow. This could be one of those times.

BIRTH NUMBER 3 – DATE NUMBER 4

SUNDAY

If you are a woman, be especially conscious right now of the dangers of 'being in love with love'. Males of this number should realise that good listeners are often more appreciated than good talkers.

MONDAY

If a matter of property or some major purchase is currently a preoccupation, your sense of values is likely to prove accurate. Don't let yourself be carried away by other people's over-enthusiasm.

TUESDAY

Avoid any tendency to flirt. Someone may take you more seriously than you intend.

WEDNESDAY

Your liking for the unusual may be satisfied if you go out of your way to cultivate a person or persons outside your normal social orbit.

THURSDAY

You could be closer than you think to pulling off a coup. However, over-hasty action may throw everything into jeopardy.

FRIDAY

Your present task may give you little pleasure but, if you abandon it, are you prepared to accept the waste of time and effort that this implies? A rest, however, could be just the thing to recharge your batteries.

SATURDAY

You're very sociable, but the hand of friendship extended to all and sundry can place burdens on others in the family. Take heed of any accusations of selfishness. They may well be very near the mark.

BIRTH NUMBER 3 – DATE NUMBER 5

SUNDAY

Friends are very important to you, but avoid the temptation to meddle in things which, strictly speaking, don't concern you. You probably don't know the full facts and you could do more harm than good.

MONDAY

Your yearning for excitement and adventure may lead you down some interesting but dangerous paths. Don't be surprised, though, if you encounter a few dead ends too. Life is full of disappointments.

TUESDAY

Use your considerable powers of imagination to develop ideas, but in applying them avoid the irrational. You sometimes get carried away by your own brilliance!

WEDNESDAY

Someone's undoubted charms may cast a spell over you, but don't let yourself be led where you don't really want to go.

THURSDAY

You seem to have taken on the mantle of prophet. If you're to be taken seriously, be certain your predictions are based on hard facts and logical analysis. Otherwise your reputation could suffer.

FRIDAY

You may be willing to try anything once, but a pet scheme could be heading for trouble if you overdo your liking for the unconventional.

SATURDAY

Cultural interests have a high profile among family or friends at the moment, but some people just want to put their feet up. You had better decide which camp you belong to.

BIRTH NUMBER 3 – DATE NUMBER 6

SUNDAY

Apathy may have led you to delay much needed changes to your home environment. Get a move on while the wherewithal is still available.

MONDAY

Your name is a byword for popularity, but people could start to give you a wide berth if your current hangdog air of depression persists. Whatever your problems, don't let them show.

TUESDAY

Words can be seductive, and someone's eloquence could be very enticing. Don't get too carried away. What is right for one person isn't necessarily right for another.

WEDNESDAY

Concentrate on solving one problem at a time. You'll achieve far more than by casting about for a single master stroke aimed at accomplishing a minor miracle.

THURSDAY

You've had your head in the sand of late, showing a disinclination to meet head-on the legitimate aspirations of those closest to you. Stop running away from the issues and make a real effort to reconcile differing points of view.

FRIDAY

People like you even when they laugh at you. This means that you can get away with a lot in life. However there is a limit to the patience of those in authority over you.

SATURDAY

Neighbours may be helpful, but make a mental note to reciprocate at an early date.

BIRTH NUMBER 3 – DATE NUMBER 7

SUNDAY

Your vision of the future, apparently founded on a rejection of beliefs you once held but which no longer seem valid, may be a little over the top. There's always something of value in the past, and much to be learnt from it.

MONDAY

The satisfaction you derive from a job well done could be spoiled by petty spite. A dignified bearing is your best defence.

TUESDAY

If you are facing an interview in the near future you should be absolutely sure that you have made adequate preparation.

WEDNESDAY

There may be friction socially, but your powers of diplomacy can help to defuse the situation. In particular, a refusal to take things too seriously can be very disarming.

THURSDAY

Doing what you like doing rather than what you should do is no way to make friends and influence people. Isn't it time you changed course?

FRIDAY

You are a generous sort. To some extent you give to others even when this means impoverishing yourself. But you're not a saint either, and you could be feeling that your kindness is being taken for granted. Make certain you're not misreading the situation before taking any irrevocable step.

SATURDAY

Domestic problems may arise through inaction or a waste of resources. Fulfil all your obligations and cut your coat according to your cloth.

BIRTH NUMBER 3 – DATE NUMBER 8

SUNDAY
You really shouldn't have to act as umpire in family squabbles. Let others settle things for themselves.

MONDAY
Avoid making statements of future intent. The more you commit yourself, the more others will expect you to come up with goods. Make your plans, keep quiet and bide your time.

TUESDAY
If someone lets you in on what is supposed to be a secret, keep it to yourself. Do absolutely nothing that could muddy the waters.

WEDNESDAY
Your current unpredictability is causing others to question your judgement. Sort out your ideas and stick to them. People want to know exactly where you stand.

THURSDAY
There are always choices in love and life. Have you finally decided where you want to go? It's time to leave the waiting room and board the train.

FRIDAY
An old proverb says that lending money may lose you a friend, whereas the refusal of a loan may keep him. The truth of this may be tested now or in the near future.

SATURDAY
Good food, good drink and good company are among your greatest pleasures, but you may have been over-indulging recently. Be a little stricter with yourself.

BIRTH NUMBER 3 – DATE NUMBER 9

SUNDAY

'Off with the old, and on with the new' seems to have been your motto for quite some time, and you appear to regard the traditional way of doing things as a sign of staleness among those around you. But change for change's sake is never a serious option.

MONDAY

Get something off your chest before someone else spills the beans.

TUESDAY

You're in such good form today that you are tempted to get involved in several schemes, each of which really requires your full attention. Beware of going off at tangents or getting side-tracked.

WEDNESDAY

If you are to get ahead in the coming weeks, it will have to be by your own unaided efforts. Expect no favours.

THURSDAY

New friends seem to have a lot to offer, but you feel bound by old loyalties. A gradual shift might be the best way to move on and also satisfy the dictates of your conscience.

FRIDAY

You may be wondering why someone doesn't seem to like you. The answer could be that you yourself are antagonistic to them. Why?

SATURDAY

Put your domestic problems on hold for the time being and make a deliberate attempt to enjoy yourself. Anyone spending a few days away from home could be in for a surprise.

BIRTH NUMBER 4 – DATE NUMBER 1

SUNDAY

Flashes of insight into the true reality of life are rare indeed, but if you can recognise the timeless fundamentals hidden deep below the humdrum surface of everyday events, there's no limit to what can be achieved. This might mean throwing off the shackles of past and present modes of thought. If so, you will have to live dangerously for a while.

MONDAY

Though your intuition could have been well off key recently, now is the time to back a hunch to the hilt. But only go ahead if you're sure wishful thinking isn't giving you a false sense of security.

TUESDAY

Mixing with people younger than yourself may help you to realise that a carefree approach to life is one you might emulate in a number of ways.

WEDNESDAY

You may make a startling discovery. If you decide to take advantage of it for your own gain, be sure that you can live with the moral dilemma this might involve.

THURSDAY

The atmosphere at home is claustrophobic. Jump at any chance to widen your horizons a little.

FRIDAY

Idealism and misplaced optimism could combine to cloud your judgement. You need to take a much more detached view of recent developments.

SATURDAY

A look through the family photograph album will reassure you about the continuity of life, despite any current sorrow or regret.

BIRTH NUMBER 4 – DATE NUMBER 2

SUNDAY

Your appetite for life seems diminished at the moment. This could be because your need for affection, understanding or recognition is being frustrated in some way. You certainly can't turn the clock back, so don't dwell on the past. Try to use your existing emotional and material assets as a foundation on which to build for the future.

MONDAY

A woman's wiles may lead you on a wild goose chase at work, so if you allow yourself to be dragged into office politics, be prepared to accept the consequences. Stay aloof, however, and no one can lead you up the garden path.

TUESDAY

Try not to bring work home with you. A hobby you may have been neglecting recently could repay renewed interest and enable you to relax in a refreshing way.

WEDNESDAY

Don't despise small beginnings. They could be the start of something big.

THURSDAY

Mixing business and pleasure is traditionally a recipe for trouble, but on this occasion the combination has a lot going for you and your ambitions.

FRIDAY

There's sometimes a fine line between self-control and inhibition. Make sure you recognise the distinction in your own actions. Otherwise you may not do yourself justice.

SATURDAY

If you have romantic problems at this time, it's probably because you're inclined to be a bit too earnest about the whole thing. A free and easy approach on the other hand might just get you where you want to be.

BIRTH NUMBER 4 – DATE NUMBER 3

SUNDAY

Oddball characters could teach you a thing or two. You may not be too keen on their general deportment, but no one is too old to learn something new, including you.

MONDAY

Remember your weaknesses as well as your strengths before taking any decisive, new step. You may lack imagination, but you have a large fund of good sense. The latter is the best barometer for future action. In the cold light of day you will surely wake up to the implausibility of wild schemes.

TUESDAY

You're not very good at delegation. Trust people whom you know to be reliable. With more of the routine off your shoulders, you can then concentrate on bigger things.

WEDNESDAY

Try out new ideas on the domestic front. If you're set in your ways, this won't be easy, but a few innovations here and there could make all the difference to the quality of life.

THURSDAY

If you're making no headway with a current project, it's probably your methods that are wrong, not the original concept. When conventional procedures fail, only an experimental approach is left.

FRIDAY

Excessive worry about your health could be misplaced, but complacency may also be misguided.

SATURDAY

If you're on an economy drive, don't get too fanatical about it. It isn't worth driving everyone, including yourself, to distraction for a few pounds saved here and there.

BIRTH NUMBER 4 – DATE NUMBER 4

SUNDAY

If old-fashioned social taboos seem to stand in your way, ignore them. An irreverent attitude could enable you to advance in directions where you have regrettably made too little progress up to now.

MONDAY

You can't afford to be too dogmatic just now. There's too much at stake for you to try and force your own ideas through without discussion and possible modification. You know very well that you, like everyone else, are never 100% right all the time.

TUESDAY

You could be in for a surprise soon. Be prepared to act in a tolerant way if it isn't exactly to your liking.

WEDNESDAY

You feel up against it at the moment, but could it be that 'it' is none other than yourself? Think about it.

THURSDAY

A simple stratagem may be all that's needed to unwind a complicated emotional struggle. You could be in such a state that you're overlooking the obvious.

FRIDAY

'All work and no play makes Jack a dull boy'. Get in the mood to spread your wings socially. You will be received with unexpected warmth.

SATURDAY

If you are being excessively selfish, you can hardly expect people to run to your aid when things go wrong. You're sensitive to the feelings of others, but sometimes not sensitive enough.

BIRTH NUMBER 4 – DATE NUMBER 5

SUNDAY

Now might be the time to examine critically the value you put on cash generally. Is money really the most important thing in the world? You may have thought so once, but a reappraisal could lead you to some interesting conclusions.

MONDAY

Be realistic about what you can achieve in the short term, and don't try to run before you can walk where new projects are concerned. It's still early days.

TUESDAY

Someone in your circle has tunnel vision, and sees only an immediate threat to their own interests, with no thought of the wider implications for everybody else. If you're in the firing line, don't fall into the trap of agreeing in principle just to reach a compromise.

WEDNESDAY

Politics – national, local or personal – preoccupy you. You may have to concede important points to get most of what you really want, whilst accommodating the other side's point of view.

THURSDAY

A surprise package in the form of a letter or phone call will need careful handling. Your initial reaction will determine the course of events, so consider every option. You won't get the chance to change your mind later on.

FRIDAY

If you're in control of events, avoid using your power for selfish or unworthy ends. Otherwise the situation could blow up in your face.

SATURDAY

Don't confuse justifiable pride with vain self-congratulation. The latter is out of place in all areas of your life.

BIRTH NUMBER 4 – DATE NUMBER 6

SUNDAY
It could be that you feel life is passing you by in important ways. If so, the old saying about living for today and letting tomorrow take care of itself is definitely relevant.

MONDAY
You may be losing valuable points in the career game, but you probably have a card or two still up your sleeve. Make sure you play them at exactly the right time.

TUESDAY
In your present mood, finding yourself on the receiving end of a hard luck story is likely to try your patience. But a sympathetic ear will cost you nothing. You may make a friend, or turn a good friend into a better one.

WEDNESDAY
Knowing what makes other people tick is a priceless advantage if you have the knack. Most of us don't, but has it occurred to you that no one appears to others as they do to themselves? Try to see behind the public mask of colleagues. You might pick out some useful points you missed before.

THURSDAY
Happiness is elusive, but you're on the right track. You know what you want. Also, you're aware that things accomplished by hard work and perseverance bring the greatest personal fulfilment.

FRIDAY
This coming weekend a shopping trip, going to a sporting event, or a night on the town can put a spring in your step. The main thing is to get out and about. If this is in the company of good friends, so much the better.

SATURDAY
Your realism sometimes has a stifling effect on the more imaginative ideas of others. Try to indulge people a little more.

BIRTH NUMBER 4 – DATE NUMBER 7

SUNDAY

You would probably agree that the image you project is a dull one. Why not show people that the real you is altogether more vibrant?

MONDAY

Jealousy may sour the atmosphere. If others attribute your happiness or success to luck, that's up to them. You have no reason to apologise for the advantages you enjoy.

TUESDAY

Some people may be sending out distress signals over an important project. You will need to understand their motivations if you decide to lend a hand, for it could be that you don't have the slightest inkling of what they are really up to.

WEDNESDAY

Recent reckless acts are quite out of character. Turn over a new leaf and look before you leap.

THURSDAY

You regard yourself as a perfectionist, and if an unsatisfactory situation has arisen, you might not be prepared to let things slide. But if you insist on decisive action right away, are you really prepared to accept all the consequences?

FRIDAY

Money in the bank is all very well, but financial caution can be overdone. Don't defer necessary purchases, and give yourself and your loved ones a treat now and then.

SATURDAY

Feelings are running high in the family circle, but a short fuse could trigger an explosion that could easily be avoided. You're not the only one who is absolutely convinced that they're right.

BIRTH NUMBER 4 – DATE NUMBER 8

SUNDAY
Even fun seems burdened with responsibility and worry! Don't be afraid to be superficial when you are supposed to be enjoying yourself.

MONDAY
No one likes injustice, and if your sense of fair play is offended, you may be inclined to feel bitter. That will only make matters worse. An opportunity to even the score will arise later on.

TUESDAY
People may be telling you to take a break. They could be right. All your recent sacrifices may be wasted if your judgement is affected by stress or strain.

WEDNESDAY
Tension will ease after a minor upheaval, but clearing away the debris may not be easy. One quick, decisive stoke is what's needed to make the whole episode just a memory.

THURSDAY
A lot of trivial, though necessary, chores could crop up unexpectedly, but don't neglect the important jobs. Establish an order of priorities.

FRIDAY
There is comparatively little risk at the moment if you seem inclined to throw your habitual caution to the winds. However, are you absolutely certain you know what you want to achieve?

SATURDAY
Have you been neglecting someone close lately? If so, there could be an almighty explosion on the way unless you take steps to repair whatever damage has been done.

BIRTH NUMBER 4 – DATE NUMBER 9

SUNDAY

A period of prosperity is in the offing, but only if you make the fullest use of your opportunities. There are dangers in over-reliance on preconceived ideas.

MONDAY

Don't expect other people to do things for you which you wouldn't do for them. There are limits to friendship.

TUESDAY

Where members of the opposite sex are concerned, concentrate on the spiritual rather than physical side of relationships.

WEDNESDAY

Facts not ideas interest you. If data is needed for some important project, insist that you get it. Don't be fobbed off with fancy theories.

THURSDAY

Changes are on the way at home. Whether major or minor, make sure you're aware of the full consequences of any commitment you make.

FRIDAY

You are devoted to order and method in all things. This is both a virtue and a vice. By all means adhere to the systematic approach, but your obsessive attention to the minutest detail means that you miss out on many of the bigger opportunities. Strategy is frequently more important than tactics.

SATURDAY

You are generally regarded as a force for stability, so any indulgence in emotional fireworks will really put the cat among the pigeons. However passionately you feel, keep calm.

BIRTH NUMBER 5 – DATE NUMBER 1

SUNDAY

Going over the events of the last year in your mind could provide a golden opportunity to re-think your ideas on quite a few strands in your life. However, don't expect to find an automatic cure for every ill.

MONDAY

Sacrifices may be in vain if others are willing to settle for less. You may have to consider breaking a dangerous connection entirely.

TUESDAY

Work is just a game really, a very serious one but a game all the same, played to rules and conventions like any other game. You can turn the rules to your advantage if you formulate the right game plan. A 'softly, softly' approach might enable you to exploit an unusual situation which seems about to develop.

WEDNESDAY

Make travel plans if you must, but really life is full of interest – even adventure – on your own doorstep, if only you take the time and trouble to look.

THURSDAY

Look for ways to widen your circle of acquaintances. You're in the mood for a good time, and new people could have a lot to offer. You've been a stick-in-the-mud for too long.

FRIDAY

Present certainty is a much more reliable asset than future hope. A large measure of the former infused with just a dash of the latter is the right combination when formulating plans.

SATURDAY

As a civilised human being you know very well that love implies responsibility. Perhaps you have been forgetting this of late. If so, now is the time to mend your ways and a lot of broken emotional fences in the process.

BIRTH NUMBER 5 – DATE NUMBER 2

SUNDAY

The mass of conflicting advice coming your way is really no help at all. At the end of the day you will have to make up your own mind on where to go from here. The inclinations of your heart over your head are worth serious consideration.

MONDAY

Your powers of persuasion are considerable. Use them to good purpose, but don't expect people to be taken in indefinitely if your ends are purely selfish.

TUESDAY

Someone very close may have temporarily lost their way. If they want to get something off their chest, be prepared to listen without preaching. Your own halo may be more than a little askew.

WEDNESDAY

You may be involved in an important meeting or series of meetings. A lot of foresight on someone's part will be needed to avoid significant errors, for the majority view could be suspect in the first instance.

THURSDAY

If you're in the midst of renovation or redecoration, you could be heading for a conflict between ideas and what is practical. The sooner you accept the realities of the situation, the better.

FRIDAY

A sudden, dramatic piece of news may be a barrier to progress. Accept the situation and prepare to move in another direction. You might even have to reverse a little before going forward.

SATURDAY

A comparative stranger on the edge of your life should stay there. Sooner or later you'll probably find out why.

BIRTH NUMBER 5 – DATE NUMBER 3

SUNDAY

By all means take risks to achieve romantic fulfilment, but if you leave yourself too vulnerable, there could be a few unforeseen consequences.

MONDAY

You're very optimistic about the future, but keep fantasies firmly in their place. It's human nature to want what you can't have. Don't be surprised if events wipe that sunny smile off your face.

TUESDAY

Laying false trails to deceive rivals may not be quite as good an idea as it seems. Should they tumble to what is going on, you could be paid back with interest. Your own position is far from unassailable.

WEDNESDAY

There's a time and a place for the distractions provided by the opposite sex, but at the moment you need to concentrate on less pleasurable matters which definitely require your undivided attention.

THURSDAY

For women there may be a conflict between the need for sensual satis-faction and the longing for security. If so, having it both ways could be an impossibility for the time being. Men who are currently playing the field are heading for complications which could see their long-term happiness sacrificed on the altar of short-term gratification.

FRIDAY

The best way to eliminate your enemies is to let them eliminate each other. Play a waiting game.

SATURDAY

If you feel your life is a bit of a mess right now, it's likely that only one real problem is at the heart of all your discontent. Go all out to solve that and everything else should pale into insignificance.

BIRTH NUMBER 5 – DATE NUMBER 4

SUNDAY

Daydreams can sometimes be productive if accompanied by a flash of intuition. Any strong conviction arising out of this process should definitely be acted upon, even if it runs contrary to conventional wisdom.

MONDAY

A lot is going on which isn't easy to explain, but your own position is secure enough provided you keep up a confident front.

TUESDAY

If you're preoccupied with romance or an emotional bond, someone older and wiser than yourself can give you the benefit of their experience.

WEDNESDAY

Someone who seldom seeks out your company seems anxious for more contact all of a sudden. You should definitely ask yourself whether there is something you aren't aware of.

THURSDAY

Let the temperature cool before you take irrevocable steps in response to words uttered in the heat of the moment.

FRIDAY

You may be confronted by an important choice. Making the right decision will depend on conquering the irrational impulses we are all prey to at times.

SATURDAY

If an announcement by someone in the family is cause for celebration, don't be surprised if you become more deeply involved than you would have anticipated.

BIRTH NUMBER 5 – DATE NUMBER 5

SUNDAY

You can look back on recent achievements with justifiable pride, but where do you go from here? An unusual source of inspiration may provide the answer. Keep your eyes and ears open.

MONDAY

Most people know your true worth, so any attempt to damage your reputation will fail. Don't retaliate. Be your usual, even-handed, competent self and your position will be strengthened.

TUESDAY

Don't postpone writing a letter or making a telephone call which is already long overdue. Someone is waiting to hear from you.

WEDNESDAY

Be very careful about those to whom you entrust even the most trivial secrets. Some people have a way of blowing things up out of all proportion to their true significance.

THURSDAY

You may lose or gain from a brush with authority. Either way, you will learn an important lesson.

FRIDAY

Recent threats to your progress in the career stakes may have receded for the present. However the danger isn't past. Stay on your guard.

SATURDAY

It's not easy to keep everyone happy today. But though some may be feeling low, your own preoccupations seem to require all your time. Spare a thought for others.

BIRTH NUMBER 5 – DATE NUMBER 6

SUNDAY

You could be feeling the prisoner of your own unfulfilled desires. Don't stumble around in the dark. Try theorising from the general to the particular, preferably in the company of someone close. No need for a formal brainstorming session, just mull things over in a relaxed setting. An escape route for the future may be revealed.

MONDAY

You may be inclined to exaggerate just now. Don't. Important contacts want to know the truth, not an embroidered version of it.

TUESDAY

It's vital to clear up misunderstandings which are holding you back. You've always made a point of trying to remain on good terms with people you don't particularly like, and once again your inclination is to shirk the issues. It would be far better to bite the bullet and get things out in the open, regardless of any offence that might be taken.

WEDNESDAY

Don't let memories of past misfortunes dog you when it comes to grasping a present opportunity. The omens are much more favourable now.

THURSDAY

A period of financial retrenchment is sound strategy at this time. Any expensive travel plans may have to be deferred or even abandoned altogether. Be realistic.

FRIDAY

There are signs of disturbance emotionally. Secretly you fancy yourself as a bit of a sexual predator, but in your heart of hearts you know the value of commitment. Be yourself and forget the fantasies.

SATURDAY

You can fool most of the people most of the time, but bottling up personal feelings is counter-productive. Try wearing your heart on your sleeve.

BIRTH NUMBER 5 – DATE NUMBER 7

SUNDAY

This is a good day for reading or study. Even recreational reading may provide an unusual insight into something of special interest to you.

MONDAY

You could find yourself in a no-win situation with a lot of personal prestige at stake. Recent mistakes may have contributed to your difficulties. A discreet veil of silence will serve you better than a premature attempt to make excuses.

TUESDAY

Be wary of 'friends' who hide their real intentions behind a social mask.

WEDNESDAY

Attending to routine may be irksome, but you certainly can't afford to let things slide in this department. Glamorous projects and exciting challenges will have their day soon enough.

THURSDAY

It may be make or break time in a relationship. One false move by you could lead to an outcome not in keeping with your true desires.

FRIDAY

Your best safeguard against bad vibrations is a determination not to be diverted from your chosen path. Let yourself be pulled this way and that by contrary impulses, and you will lose ground.

SATURDAY

Family undercurrents may be about to well up into a major confrontation. Domestic intrigues probably leave you cold in your present mood, but intervention now will save you no end of trouble in the long run.

BIRTH NUMBER 5 – DATE NUMBER 8

SUNDAY
Time marches on and few things remain exactly the same, especially people. A long, hard look at those around you may cause you to revise your opinion of some individuals. This will affect how you handle them in the future.

MONDAY
Don't be taken in by flattery. You need to keep your head out of the clouds and your feet planted firmly on the ground if you're to emerge triumphant in the days ahead.

TUESDAY
Some things are better left unsaid. Remember that, if some people don't see your point of view.

WEDNESDAY
A backlog of routine chores which have accumulated over the weeks may be crying out for attention. Set to work with a will. When you've done what is necessary, sit back and relax. You will have earned a good rest.

THURSDAY
Other people's intransigence may be standing in your way. Try to understand the reasons for their stubborn attitude. But you, like everyone else, are better at giving advice than receiving it, so resist any temptation to lay down the law.

FRIDAY
Honesty as the best policy is not always an easy one to adopt, especially in those areas of life where black and white mingle. But if you keep your own integrity intact at this time, you could get a tangible reward.

SATURDAY
Don't give up if things are especially tough at the moment. There's light at the end of the tunnel.

BIRTH NUMBER 5 – DATE NUMBER 9

SUNDAY

If you are feeling you're going the wrong way in important areas of your life, ask yourself who is in the driving seat. If the honest answer is 'Not me', then it's time you got your hands back on the steering wheel and took charge of your own destiny.

MONDAY

Someone may make a point in a friendly sort of way which could be interpreted as criticism. Don't fly off the handle. There might be a lot in what they say.

TUESDAY

If you're unprepared to commit yourself emotionally, try to understand why. Face facts and play the game with all concerned, including yourself.

WEDNESDAY

Life may be monotonous at times, but the remedy is in your own hands. For instance, a different kind of holiday this year could be just the lift you need.

THURSDAY

A delicate situation will require careful handling if you are not to lose ground in a matter which is definitely not marginal where your personal happiness is concerned. However a moral victory alone may not satisfy you.

FRIDAY

Last minute preparations for a social event may call for all your attention, so don't skimp. Any backsliding could find you out in an embarrassing way. Beware of eavesdroppers later in the day.

SATURDAY

Unless you thrive on conflict, members of the opposite sex with a strong will and a mind of their own are not really for you, whatever their physical charms. Right now you need some sympathy and a lot of understanding.

BIRTH NUMBER 6 – DATE NUMBER 1

SUNDAY

It may be that your dull old world just doesn't conform to your high expectations. But expectations have to be translated into action if you are to live successfully. Stop shooting at the moon and get on with something real and attainable.

MONDAY

If you're on your mettle, you could come across a lost possession unexpectedly. Or someone from the past may suddenly reappear.

TUESDAY

Secrecy may bring you good fortune, provided others stand to benefit also.

WEDNESDAY

You have changed your mind a hundred times lately. This outward inconsistency is a reflection of inner turmoil. Whatever the cause of the latter, it will have to be dispelled before you can go forward in the knowledge of what your real priorities are.

THURSDAY

You're in an indulgent mood. Others may find you an excellent companion, but you may be letting things slide too much when it comes to your own vital interests.

FRIDAY

Men who find the female mentality totally unfathomable should avoid asking questions and allow mysteries to remain just that. Women must be wary of men whose sincerity may be in doubt.

SATURDAY

There are a host of opportunities on the horizon along with a series of options about how to make the best use of them. Don't err on the side of caution. Fortune favours a bold stroke.

BIRTH NUMBER 6 – DATE NUMBER 2

SUNDAY

Recent mistakes were mainly due to the fact that you're inclined to act first and think later, especially under pressure. Also, short cuts attract you and you enjoy flirting with danger. All these impulses should be kept in check before your next decisive step.

MONDAY

There are times when you deliberately take refuge in ambiguity. This ploy might not work the next time you try to talk your way out of a tight corner.

TUESDAY

You have taken some hard knocks, but you do seem a lot tougher these days. However people can have long memories. Where there are mountains to climb, you will need to assert yourself as never before to convince others that you really mean business.

WEDNESDAY

Love is in the air, but much more than a candlelit dinner and a bunch of flowers is needed. Real life unfortunately isn't like a romantic novel.

THURSDAY

Doing the right thing in a complex situation may be much more difficult than you anticipate. Don't fudge the issue. Decide where you stand and accept the consequences. Whatever you do, you could easily come out smelling of roses.

FRIDAY

No one can seriously damage your position at this time, though in the 'rat race', watching your back is only common sense.

SATURDAY

Don't make promises you know you can't keep.

BIRTH NUMBER 6 – DATE NUMBER 3

SUNDAY

There's never a dull moment in the weeks ahead, mainly because you're suddenly bursting with energy. But you may find that not everyone wants to be swept along on the tide of your boundless enthusiasm.

MONDAY

You may achieve a step forward in your career, but don't imagine everything is due to your own cleverness. Luck and the goodwill of others may have contributed too. Become complacent or conceited, and the very influences which were working in your favour could swing in the opposite direction.

TUESDAY

There are two sorts of people – givers and takers. Whether you like it or not, you have to get along with both.

WEDNESDAY

Do your feelings towards people veer sharply from affection to indifference? A recent disappointment may be the cause. Put it behind you, and be happy in the company of those you like and who like you.

THURSDAY

You're always on the move, constantly searching for new angles or fresh possibilities. Fine, but put the finishing touches to what you've started before chasing off in some new direction.

FRIDAY

Friends seem intent on saying the opposite of what they mean. Plain speaking by you will help to clear the air, but don't expect everyone to agree with you about everything.

SATURDAY

Mechanical problems around the house are vexing, but keep a sense of proportion. Try to be philosophical. Giving in to stress is so unproductive.

BIRTH NUMBER 6 – DATE NUMBER 4

SUNDAY

The niche you've carved out for yourself in life so far suits you very well, but if your love of beauty and the finer things gives rise to vague, unfulfilled longings, there's still much you can do even without a princely income. Your discernment and good taste can take you down the path you wish to travel.

MONDAY

This is not a good day to push too hard. Procrastination, far from being the thief of time, is a sound tactic just now. It could steer you away from negative influences until the moment arrives for a positive surge.

TUESDAY

Don't rely too much on other people, don't jump to conclusions, and do think before you speak or act. If things get difficult, try to melt into the background. There will be better days for a bold approach.

WEDNESDAY

An accident or a loss is indicated. Its nature or extent isn't clear, but you can be a tower of strength for others, whatever your inner emotions.

THURSDAY

It could be that you have too many fingers in too many pies. Refine your goals and focus on a course of action which is likely to achieve them.

FRIDAY

In the past you may have been taken in by people who make promises but rarely keep them. Don't repeat the mistake in the future.

SATURDAY

There is an opportunity for travel now or in the not too distant future, but however much you like the idea in theory, practical considerations will have to be borne in mind. Partner's or family reaction are important too. Don't act in haste.

BIRTH NUMBER 6 – DATE NUMBER 5

SUNDAY
Married people or those in a long-term relationship should be clear in their own minds whether shared or separate interests have a priority just now.

MONDAY
Everyone is in a rush today. You, on the other hand, definitely need a pause for thought. If you can coast along without getting too involved, this will give you the breathing space you want.

TUESDAY
Should a surprise development throw literally everything into the melting pot, defer action to another day, provided there's no chance of someone stealing a march on you.

WEDNESDAY
Try not to be so easily swayed by people you admire. What's good for others isn't necessarily right for you.

THURSDAY
Spend any sudden windfall as fast as you can. Indulge yourself this once, and the resulting boost will be much better for you than brooding over a possible rainy day.

FRIDAY
Hard-liners seem to be getting the upper hand at work, and your more moderate approach is out of favour. You might not be willing to swim with the tide, but don't get too far away from the shore either.

SATURDAY
If you're thinking of additions to your wardrobe, most fashion experts would agree that being smart is a combination of elegance and simplicity. This is true whatever your budget.

BIRTH NUMBER 6 – DATE NUMBER 6

SUNDAY
There may be obstacles to do with love, money or work, but a fatalistic attitude is wrong. You can control events more than you realise.

MONDAY
Don't rely on colleagues, friends or even family to volunteer the whole truth. You may have to find out some things for yourself. Certainly not everything is as it seems.

TUESDAY
Quick reactions will be needed to keep a lot of balls in the air simultaneously. The juggling act may include possession of a secret that will keep a little longer, so cool it.

WEDNESDAY
If you go out in the evening, a chance meeting might stir up unpleasant memories. Rather than spoil what should have been a good day, a quiet evening at home could be the best way of rounding things off.

THURSDAY
You're in danger of being pulled all over the place by contrary influences. You know very well that you can't have your cake and eat it too, so decide on your best option and forget everything else.

FRIDAY
The numbers suggest that calculation and idealism currently motivate you in equal proportions. It's unlikely the split can continue much longer.

SATURDAY
Dreams of what might have been are a waste of time. Where you go from here should be your only consideration.

BIRTH NUMBER 6 – DATE NUMBER 7

SUNDAY

The omens are far from good for a successful day. Unless you get a firm grip on events early on, it could be that by the time it's over you'll be wishing you hadn't bothered to get out of bed.

MONDAY

A missed opportunity may have a 'domino' effect in the morning, or a lucky encounter could pay an unusual dividend after lunch. Accidental events like this are a symptom of just how important a factor chance is in your life at the moment.

TUESDAY

There's a lot of opposition from some members of the family to your domestic plans. They can be talked round, the more so as your ideas are fundamentally sound.

WEDNESDAY

Suspicion could be casting a shadow over your emotional life. If you continue to withhold your trust, don't be surprised if current strains develop into an ever-widening rift.

THURSDAY

You may be feeling on top of the world, but the obstacles to your progress are still there, despite your buoyant mood. Don't let frustration put a sharp edge on your tongue.

FRIDAY

A skeleton could pop out of the family cupboard. With luck the resulting trauma will be mild and short-lived. Distance yourself from the whole business as far as possible.

SATURDAY

If things have gone a little flat in a relationship recently, you need to find new ways to break the cycle of familiar routine that can so easily bedevil shared experience.

BIRTH NUMBER 6 – DATE NUMBER 8

SUNDAY

A crisis may be looming. Fortunately you're in the mood to tackle anything, but beware of being swept away on a tide of recrimination. Accept your share of the blame, if any, and no more.

MONDAY

Whatever sort of day it turns out to be, give yourself a lift with a little of what you fancy. Should this involve another person, you will be gratified to discover that they have much the same thing in mind.

TUESDAY

Any really decisive, major step should be deferred until after your next birthday. Facts bearing on the situation will be much clearer by then.

WEDNESDAY

If you are not currently in paid employment, involvement in community projects will give you a sense of worth and bolster your self-esteem. People in work should act charitably.

THURSDAY

You will continue to be an inspiration to others, provided you remain confident of your own abilities and the rightness of your aims. This is no time for self-doubt.

FRIDAY

You may be powerless if things take a turn for the worse quite soon. Accept the inevitable, but that doesn't mean you can't find some good in the situation to take with you into the future.

SATURDAY

Things are much calmer at home now, but you still feel restricted by circumstances beyond your control. Be patient.

BIRTH NUMBER 6 – DATE NUMBER 9

SUNDAY

Significant changes may have taken place in your life recently, but it may be quite some time before their full effects begin to work through to your daily routine. In the meantime take the rough with the smooth.

MONDAY

Though your abilities may be greater than some of your colleagues', retain a healthy respect for the contribution they make. You will suffer if you gain a reputation for arrogance.

TUESDAY

A few simple improvements can increase the quality of external life without overtaxing your resources. Some subtle colour changes might make all the difference. Also, home security arrangements could repay attention.

WEDNESDAY

If you're to encounter misfortune, it probably won't be as bad as you fear. Even so there is no room for complacency.

THURSDAY

Old friends will be happy to see you if you've neglected them of late. As a result, little niggles at home and at work will pale into insignificance in the general air of bonhomie.

FRIDAY

What you really need to boost morale is some kind of striking success. But spectacular gains seldom arrive to order. Perseverance combined with a cautious optimism should bring a reward in the end.

SATURDAY

You may be disinclined to venture very far from your own door. So what? Relax in the way that suits your mood.

BIRTH NUMBER 7 – DATE NUMBER 1

SUNDAY

It will do you no good at all if you retreat into a dream world and pretend your problems don't exist. Await developments and avoid rocking the boat. Possible solutions will emerge from a calm appreciation of the facts.

MONDAY

You're in a discursive mood. If your advice is sought during a casual conversation, your standing as a counsellor could rise with someone who needs an impartial view.

TUESDAY

If your present task seems a thankless one, a word to a colleague or a superior might produce some extra help. Feelings pent up for too long could easily drag you into a no-win situation of frustration and despair.

WEDNESDAY

You seem to be carrying around a lot of emotional baggage. It's time to decide what really matters where your feelings are concerned and throw everything else away.

THURSDAY

Dreams are the mind's way of sorting out current emotional concerns, but a particularly vivid one could turn into a self-fulfilling prophecy when it comes to an unresolved situation on a conscious level.

FRIDAY

Face up to things as they really are, not as you would like them to be. Fool yourself once too often and the consequences could be disastrous.

SATURDAY

Privacy is obviously important, but opening your door, as well as your heart, a bit more often will make you a happier person.

BIRTH NUMBER 7 – DATE NUMBER 2

SUNDAY

Love and sensuality are not always the same thing. In this phase of your life, are you sure you know the difference?

MONDAY

You need to be on your guard against trickery or sharp practice at this time. The motives and actions of some people are pitched in a much lower key than your own code of ethics.

TUESDAY

If you have developed a grand strategy which you hope will get you what you want, remember that details in its execution can be just as important as the overall design.

WEDNESDAY

If you owe someone a personal favour, better to repay it early than late, and failing that, better late than never.

THURSDAY

You're something of an outsider, but to say that you are currently suffering from an identity crisis would probably be an exaggeration. But you do need to feel more secure in your public *persona*. Get involved.

FRIDAY

Absent friends could make their presence felt in a most unexpected way which will bring a lot of pleasure.

SATURDAY

If you're male and in a romantic frame of mind, you should realise that most women succumb eventually to repeated declarations of affection. Women should resist any inclination to keep their emotions under lock and key where matters of the heart are concerned.

BIRTH NUMBER 7 – DATE NUMBER 3

SUNDAY

Your tendency to daydream brings you perilously close to fantasy at times. You need to come down to earth. Your partner or a close friend might be the one to impart the necessary home truths.

MONDAY

Where the opposite sex is concerned, things are not made any easier by your excessively complicated inner life. Could it be that you don't really know what you do want? If so, then you're unlikely to get it.

TUESDAY

If you allow yourself to be pushed into the position of spokesperson, there can be no sitting on the fence. Do you really want to stand up and be counted at the moment?

WEDNESDAY

Some of your ideas have excellent potential, but you may need help to realise it. Don't go it alone.

THURSDAY

Your liking for secrecy will gain you no friends. Is it so bad if others find out more about you? They will certainly trust you more if they know you better.

FRIDAY

Stale relationships may be due for a shake-up. Only you know how much of the past you wish to endure. However, events could develop a momentum of their own, independent of your desires.

SATURDAY

You are acting like a saint, but thinking like a sinner. Whatever the temptation, it could well be a case of 'better the devil you know than the devil you don't'.

BIRTH NUMBER 7 – DATE NUMBER 4

SUNDAY

You are suffering from a conflict between material aims and spiritual values. Unless you're prepared to compromise some of your most cherished ideals, you'll just have to cut your coat according to your ethical cloth.

MONDAY

You have achieved a great deal, or at the very least prospects are good. But you seem to lack that little bit of extra confidence needed to apply the finishing touches. Don't hang back now. Give yourself the final push necessary to cash in on all your hard work.

TUESDAY

There could be a conflict over the upbringing of children, but all concerned will understand one another better if a real attempt is made to clear the air. Single people should steer clear of controversy in their relationships with parents.

WEDNESDAY

Anyone who succeeds in getting you rattled has won a victory. It may be difficult to distance yourself from petty rivalries, but try. The consequences of escalation into a head-to-head could rumble on for weeks.

THURSDAY

Playing the strong, silent type may gain you respect but few real friends. Your current style is too heavy-handed. Try to recover your sense of humour.

FRIDAY

Things are seldom as bad as they seem, and a lot of the difficulties standing in your way may well be imaginary. There's a distinction between prudence and the excessive pessimism which is paralysing your ability to make progress.

SATURDAY

You're very tense right now because of a build-up of emotions you have suppressed for too long. Perhaps an explosion would be no bad thing.

BIRTH NUMBER 7 – DATE NUMBER 5

SUNDAY

Solitary oaks grow strong, and you have a liking for being alone. This isn't always the best thing for you, but on this occasion a little solitude will do no harm at all.

MONDAY

Your creative juices are flowing, and if you meet with opposition, an unorthodox approach might be just what's needed to disarm those who are inclined to dig their heels in. You may even win applause from an unexpected quarter for a job well done.

TUESDAY

If either money or sex are troubling you, you won't be happy as long as either remains an obsession which shuts out everything else.

WEDNESDAY

Those in the housing market or with legal problems could receive good news soon. If things have got off to a slow start or on the wrong footing altogether, it may pay to get in touch with interested parties to see if progress is now possible.

THURSDAY

Your code of honour certainly doesn't allow you to ingratiate yourself with those in authority, but you do carry self-reliance too far at times. After all, no one will scratch your back unless you scratch theirs.

FRIDAY

You seem reluctant to make the first move with a member of the other sex. Remember, fear of rejection is one of the most basic of human emotions. You must decide which is worse – a blow to your pride or the possibility of a missed opportunity.

SATURDAY

Don't hesitate to call a family conference if you can't see the way out of a domestic bind. There's strength in unity.

BIRTH NUMBER 7 – DATE NUMBER 6

SUNDAY

You may discover the answer to a current problem in the very last place you would expect to find it.

MONDAY

The only way of finding out something you need to know may be to admit your ignorance, even if this means losing face.

TUESDAY

You're a good loser, but you don't have to be a loser at all if only you could learn to concentrate on essentials. Forget all about straws in the wind and go for the main chance. Today is a good day to start being a winner!

WEDNESDAY

For those in contact with 'High-Tech', the apparent shortcomings of technology may be no more than a symptom of a lack of understanding on your part. Don't be afraid to seek out the advice of those who are supposed to know.

THURSDAY

Your current sedentary lifestyle isn't good for you. Make a real effort to be more physically active.

FRIDAY

You have the changeability of an overactive chameleon at the moment. You say and do one thing, but think another. The ability to manoeuvre is part of the art of living, but there are limits. Unresolved, the split in your personality could eventually prove an intolerable strain.

SATURDAY

You need to reassure yourself that you're on the right track with future plans. Your fears are groundless. The original analysis was almost certainly correct.

BIRTH NUMBER 7 – DATE NUMBER 7

SUNDAY

Doubts about the future could be a reflection of your natural pessimism rather than of any basic flaw in your position in the world. The worst will almost certainly never happen, and the best could be yet to come.

MONDAY

The job in hand may not get done if you rely on someone else to do it.

TUESDAY

If others seem to encroach on what you regard as your own personal domain, you may have to accept that even you don't have exclusive rights all the time over everything that is most important to you.

WEDNESDAY

You have a better insight than most into hidden emotional depths, and although other people's needs may be difficult to discern, now is the time to use your gift.

THURSDAY

You may feel like a pawn in a chess match at the moment, but pawns start on the front rank and can ultimately win the game.

FRIDAY

Once in a while something unexpected happens with which you are ill-equipped to deal. Today could be one of those times. Struck by a bolt from the blue, make time to think and react.

SATURDAY

True ambition is aiming to live in the way that will make you happiest. In a material world it's all too easy to forget this fact.

BIRTH NUMBER 7 – DATE NUMBER 8

SUNDAY
You're definitely vulnerable at present, not least because of your refusal to face facts. The remedy is in your own hands.

MONDAY
Salting money away is not in your nature, but any temptation to blow spare cash on an unconsidered whim should be firmly resisted.

TUESDAY
There really doesn't seem much chance of your recent efforts being converted into positive gains for the present. Keep your head down, and don't worry if you don't know everything that's going on behind the scenes. Vital information will emerge all in good time.

WEDNESDAY
You will feel happiest in those quiet moments between bursts of activity. Make sure you make the time to relax.

THURSDAY
You have never found it particularly easy to make friends, and you never will as long as you meet people with your guard up. Meeting others half-way can open many doors. Now is an excellent period for extending the hand of friendship.

FRIDAY
Self-righteousness as a cloak for obstinacy won't help anybody, including yourself. Something's got to give. It might have to be you.

SATURDAY
Everyone, even couch potatoes, benefit from a change of scene, so don't pass up an opportunity to get out and about. Those with sporting interests could get a real 'high' from a favourable result.

BIRTH NUMBER 7 – DATE NUMBER 9

SUNDAY
Time to take a long, hard look at your finances. Important adjustments may or may not be needed. Either way, a lot will depend on decisions taken now. Don't play hunches and don't gamble.

MONDAY
If you now have more power to influence events than formerly, you will know instinctively when the time is right to exercise it. Disregard external pressures to rush matters.

TUESDAY
Remembering a face and the name that goes with it is not one of your strong points. But nearly everybody responds to this form of flattery, and you should work at remedying this chink in your armour.

WEDNESDAY
If you're at something of a loose end, literature, music or some other artistic pursuit could be just the thing to tide you over a barren patch.

THURSDAY
Always try to see the best in everything, including people, but don't let your own sincerity override good sense. You can be too naive at times.

FRIDAY
There is a serious break in the lines of communication between yourself and others. Guilt about your own past conduct may be the root of the problem. You could have to do some owning up.

SATURDAY
The recent past may have been a series of mixed blessings. Since life is ups and downs in roughly equal measure, the immediate future probably won't be much different.

BIRTH NUMBER 8 – DATE NUMBER 1

SUNDAY

You currently seemed isolated on many fronts. Since others don't seem inclined to take the initiative in your direction, you need to make a determined effort in theirs.

MONDAY

Your habitual diffidence may well be due to the fact that you have yet to reach your full potential. The problem is that modesty has become ingrained and acts as a brake on your progress.

TUESDAY

The more you trust your own judgement at the moment, the better. You won't always be right, but your mistakes will be no worse than those of others who may try to influence you.

WEDNESDAY

If you want to feel fully alive, physical fitness is just as important as mental well-being. Look after your body and your mind will look after itself.

THURSDAY

Forget recent slights. Only if your forgiveness goes unheeded will it be right to consider how to retaliate.

FRIDAY

You tend to shy away from public displays of emotions both by yourself and on the part of others. But turning your back on fraught situations will only give you a reputation as someone who doesn't care. This is especially true at the present time.

SATURDAY

Children can add significantly to the general atmosphere of contentment if they are encouraged to make a contribution. Their views are important too, and should be listened to.

BIRTH NUMBER 8 – DATE NUMBER 2

SUNDAY

You can't continue in your troubled state of mind indefinitely. Whatever the cause of your anxiety, the solution lies in action, not solitary contemplation.

MONDAY

Any dramatic change could be for the worse. Be content to let things remain pretty much as they are.

TUESDAY

If you can see senior colleagues as well as your peers as part of a single family group, you will be able to focus your emotions better in the work place. Feeling like an insider, you have a much greater chance of making others appreciate your talents at their true value.

WEDNESDAY

If you are thinking of entertaining or attending a social gathering, check dates and times to avoid a possible mix-up.

THURSDAY

Cut your losses if a financial plan has turned out badly. Don't throw good money after bad.

FRIDAY

By all means diversify your interests in small ways, but don't lose sight of your main objective.

SATURDAY

It's nearly always best to talk about your feelings. Hide them and no one can help you with a sympathetic ear or active support.

BIRTH NUMBER 8 – DATE NUMBER 3

SUNDAY

Your life has arrived at something of an impasse. The cultivation of new friends or contacts may be the way out.

MONDAY

Worry for the mind, like pain for the body, is a necessary signal, warning of danger. The trouble is that you worry when you should, but also when you shouldn't. If you learn to recognise the difference, you will rid yourself of at least some of your anxiety.

TUESDAY

There's a big difference between freedom and feeling free. You have plenty of the former, and being hemmed in on all sides by people making demands on you is a common human experience. There are a lot more pluses in your life than minuses, and if this is not exactly a consolation, it should be a starting point for coping as usual.

WEDNESDAY

You could be feeling decidedly grumpy. If you allow yourself to vent your temper on others today, you will have a lot of apologising to do tomorrow.

THURSDAY

You are feeling the need to be valued for yourself, not for what you have to give. The truth is that you probably are, so don't be put out if people neglect to provide positive proof all the time.

FRIDAY

Those who suffer from headaches or insomnia should not accept that there is no remedy, however old the problem.

SATURDAY

Trouble may be brewing, but given the right attitude, it could be you who gets the good out of this particular ill wind.

BIRTH NUMBER 8 – DATE NUMBER 4

SUNDAY

Avoid crowds today. If you want a break from routine, head for the wide open spaces.

MONDAY

Don't jump to conclusions and don't bite off more than you can chew. You have a definite tendency to do both at the present time.

TUESDAY

Those in your family circle will give you a much needed boost. Resist any temptation to accept obligations which will take you away from the domestic scene.

WEDNESDAY

You are too sensitive for your own good at times. A careless remark, perhaps made in jest but without malice, may upset you where other people would hardly notice a slight at all. Try not to be so touchy.

THURSDAY

Not everyone is instantly likeable, but it may be better to reserve judgement about a newcomer in your life.

FRIDAY

One minute your smile is all sweetness and light, the next you grit your teeth in grim determination. Which facial mask reflects the real you at this stage of your development? Others are confused and, as you're not a particularly calculating person, you are probably confused as well.

SATURDAY

This is a time to think and listen. You will know when it's right to apply what you have learnt.

BIRTH NUMBER 8 – DATE NUMBER 5

SUNDAY

One of the family may be as open and upfront as ever. But appearances can be deceptive. It might not be easy to bring things out into the open. Once you know the full facts, however, you may be in a position to help.

MONDAY

You've been in something of a rut for quite some time. You always err on the conservative side and prefer to stick to what is safe and familiar. Try ringing the changes, if only in small ways.

TUESDAY

Educational matters are very important for you or your children in this phase. Some sacrifice may be called for.

WEDNESDAY

You have it all worked out how to proceed with an important project, but the unexpected could take a hand. More flexibility than you anticipated may be necessary.

THURSDAY

A fairly tough regime of diet or exercise could be beneficial. If you've already embarked on such a programme, only you will have to count the cost if you weaken now.

FRIDAY

You seem confused where a relationship is concerned. Someone is confused by your confusion. Things may reach breaking point if the situation is allowed to continue.

SATURDAY

Your fairness is something which has always drawn people to you. If difficult choices lie ahead, try to appear as impartial as possible, even if you have to come down on one side or the other.

BIRTH NUMBER 8 – DATE NUMBER 6

SUNDAY

If you are trying to win your partner over to your point of view about a pet scheme, be direct. You could find yourself accused of being insincere if you try a roundabout approach.

MONDAY

Wait until the very last moment before leaving the sidelines and coming to a final decision. The situation is complex and circumstances may alter by the minute.

TUESDAY

Your patience might be stretched to the limit, but teamwork can succeed on this occasion just as it has done in the past, even though some key people seem intent on dragging their heels.

WEDNESDAY

A critical examination of your own true motivations may enable you to make some adjustments to the image you project. Others could respond enthusiastically to the new you.

THURSDAY

You have a choice between developing your artistic abilities or concentrating on the more practical side of your nature. The latter may prove ultimately more rewarding.

FRIDAY

Platonic friendship may bring you greater happiness at this time than more romantic involvement.

SATURDAY

If you can relax off the beaten track either in terms of place or of the things you usually do, the novelty of the situation should bring its own reward.

BIRTH NUMBER 8 – DATE NUMBER 7

SUNDAY

Feeling frustrated, the best channel for your energies could be the one you have considered least. In fact your priorities generally may be in entirely the wrong order.

MONDAY

A storm is blowing up which may catch you unawares. Your best chance of riding it out with your interests intact is to throw caution to the wind and go all out for total victory.

TUESDAY

Anyone whose romantic hopes have been disappointed recently could be in the mood for self-congratulation by bed time.

WEDNESDAY

Stop suffering in silence if plagued by a minor ailment. Do something about it. The problem is unlikely to go away by itself.

THURSDAY

You're inclined to panic if things don't go well in the short term. Temporary setbacks are unavoidable. It's the final outcome that counts.

FRIDAY

Your current aspirations are attainable only if you use what you have accomplished so far as a foundation on which to build. A period of consolidation is needed. Any new and radical departure would be dangerous.

SATURDAY

The social scene beckons right now. Let yourself be drawn into the swing of things, especially where women take the lead. As a by-product of having a good time, someone's intuition could shed light on a situation which has mystified you for quite some time.

BIRTH NUMBER 8 – DATE NUMBER 8

SUNDAY

A little of what you fancy does you good, but you are taking a few liberties with more serious obligations. Try to get back to what matters most.

MONDAY

By all means go all out to achieve your immediate aims, but what seems most desirable now could be quite different to what you will really covet in a few months' time.

TUESDAY

Those in a marriage or a permanent relationship may find their partner unwilling to fall into line over social or holiday plans. A trade-off in some other area might be the only way to break the deadlock.

WEDNESDAY

You're in no mood to be trifled with. Anyone who tries to limit your freedom of action or take advantage in some way is likely to meet with stiff resistance. Be tactful however. There's no point in going over the top and causing lasting resentment.

THURSDAY

Your practical bent is and always will be one of your greatest assets. Theoretical speculation or discussion should be left to those who lack your ability to get things done or make things work.

FRIDAY

You're a long way from breaking point financially. If money matters are intricate, therefore, you'll probably be right not to fuss too much about details. All the head-scratching in the world is unlikely to produce any sudden, dramatic improvement.

SATURDAY

You're paralysed by a sense of your own limitations. Fear is too strong a word, but at the moment you do tend to hang back at times when boldness would carry the day.

BIRTH NUMBER 8 – DATE NUMBER 9

SUNDAY

Matrimonial prospects for the unmarried will be improved if a blind eye is turned to an apparent indiscretion. For them, just as for everyone else, things may not be exactly what they seem in the emotional sphere.

MONDAY

Differences of opinion are part of life, so don't take offence if someone doesn't agree with you. It might be that they have more logic on their side than you.

TUESDAY

You may have taken a detour in your career lately. If you are to get back on course, you must return to basics. Keep a sense of proportion and your mind on the job.

WEDNESDAY

If you encounter difficulties with people in offices or shops who are there to serve, remember that they don't make the rules. It's up to you to adapt to the latter if you are to make progress.

THURSDAY

A period of calm reflection is needed, so you can come to terms with the mixture of emotions that have built up recently. This doesn't mean a retreat into splendid isolation. Get on with your life at the same time.

FRIDAY

Living is a process of continuous learning, even though you may think you know all you need to know. In fact an alert, receptive mind discovers something new every day. Could that be where you've been going wrong lately?

SATURDAY

You might have cause to appreciate the truth of the saying that trouble comes in threes, although there could be a silver lining in at least one cloud.

BIRTH NUMBER 9 – DATE NUMBER 1

SUNDAY

In the sexual arena you are very susceptible to the heady brew of wanting and being wanted. However this is not always a recipe for happiness.

MONDAY

You wouldn't go from London to Edinburgh via Land's End. Why then do you persist in going all round the houses to get what you want? You're not a tourist in life, for whom time is no object. Perhaps it's simply a case of being too devious for your own good.

TUESDAY

You have great pride. The proverb tells you to watch out for a fall. You have been caught unawares in the past. Could it happen again fairly soon?

WEDNESDAY

Bargain hunters should have a field day provided cash is plentiful. If not, restraint is called for.

THURSDAY

Your aspirations are liable to take a few serious knocks if you overreach yourself at critical moments. 'Make haste slowly' ought to be your motto.

FRIDAY

Old hopes and ideals have been gathering dust in the recesses of your mind for quite a while. A sudden shaft of light may illuminate the way and show you how to revitalise former goals.

SATURDAY

You probably feel you're getting nowhere fast at the moment. You could go back to the beginning and start again, but a U-turn gives no guarantee of success, and anyway you don't really know where you went wrong in the first place. Keep going. You could win out in the end.

BIRTH NUMBER 9 – DATE NUMBER 2

SUNDAY
You may think you have just cause for feeling angry and hurt over a recent turn of events. However an explosion of wrath will do you no good at all. Crying over spilt milk is pointless too.

MONDAY
If you receive an urgent message, there may be more to it than meets the eye. Consider your next move very carefully.

TUESDAY
A vague sense of unease is gradually creeping into your outlook. The chances are that there isn't much to worry about, but you should certainly take time out to analyse your feelings.

WEDNESDAY
The ruling numbers suggest that what seems like a major domestic issue today could be just a minor one by tomorrow. All things are in a state of flux, and time has a way of unwinding even the most complicated of knots.

THURSDAY
Resist the temptation to meddle in what strictly speaking doesn't concern you. It's so easy to alienate important people.

FRIDAY
You're much too abrupt with all and sundry at present. It's one thing to have the courage of your convictions, quite another to force your opinions down other people's throats.

SATURDAY
There's no hope unless you adopt a desperate remedy for a current problem. Shilly-shallying will do more harm than good.

BIRTH NUMBER 9 – DATE NUMBER 3

SUNDAY

If you're in an amorous mood, temper your desires with a strong dash of realism. You might get what you want in the end, but impractical daydreaming is not the way to go about it.

MONDAY

Wait for it if a crisis seems to be looming. Why rush headlong into other people's trouble? You may become involved eventually, but that's by no means certain.

TUESDAY

Where legal or financial matters are concerned, pay particular attention to the small print.

WEDNESDAY

Don't lose sleep over little puzzles which you know deep down have no real importance. Some things in life will always remain a mystery.

THURSDAY

What you see as one person's, or possibly several people's, shortcomings might lead you to say things you will regret later on. It takes all sorts to make a world, and you're not perfect yourself.

FRIDAY

Your imagination is running riot today and suddenly life seems full of limitless possibilities. Your good sense will lead you to ignore, quite rightly, the more fanciful notions which flit through your mind, but an adventurous approach is definitely in tune with the times.

SATURDAY

New developments may open up an old wound. If the past has a bearing on the future, don't hesitate to take this into account when deciding what to do.

BIRTH NUMBER 9 – DATE NUMBER 4

SUNDAY

On the domestic front there's lots to be thankful for. However, those closest to you will also have played their part. If the favourable trend is to continue, avoid any sudden change of direction with which others may not be in agreement. You can be a bit too forceful on occasion.

MONDAY

A hasty career move now would be most ill-advised. Future seas could be choppy and your present haven is a safe anchorage.

TUESDAY

It may be a good idea to review arrangements with regard to insurance. Fate could soon play a trick or two not to your advantage.

WEDNESDAY

You fear betrayal, but are your own motives entirely sincere?

THURSDAY

Boredom weighs heavily on you just now. One way out of your spiritual unease is to exploit your talent for interacting with many different kinds of people, in order to open up fresh avenues for personal fulfilment.

FRIDAY

Simple precautions are all that's needed to prevent things going wrong. If others have neglected to take them, you must be the one to do so.

SATURDAY

Slow down. You have plenty of time to do everything you want in the days and weeks ahead. Rush your fences on the other hand and you might easily end up on the floor. If you do no more than is expected of you, that will be enough for now.

BIRTH NUMBER 9 – DATE NUMBER 5

SUNDAY

You may have to be cruel to be kind with a younger member of the family. Firmness now will forestall greater problems later on.

MONDAY

You could hear something that throws the future in doubt as far as your career is concerned. Be careful. Your confidant may be misinformed.

TUESDAY

Your partner could be shying away from a frank discussion that would clear the air. A tiny niggle may be causing far more discontent than it really warrants.

WEDNESDAY

You may prefer to go it alone for a while, if that's possible. This could be the right thing to do, especially if you have good reason to doubt someone's good faith.

THURSDAY

Calm and careful consideration should be the order of the day, but you are feeling reckless. Try to analyse the cause of your cavalier mood. Then you'll be much more in control.

FRIDAY

Even a strong person can be influenced by the weak at times. Don't let appeals to your better nature divert you from what is really best for you and those who depend on you.

SATURDAY

Trouble may arise from a matter touching on sexual equality. Compromise if that will solve the difficulty.

BIRTH NUMBER 9 – DATE NUMBER 6

SUNDAY

A family feud may be about to come to a head, but anyone with a sense of proportion would be asking what all the fuss is about. One well-timed joke could see all the aggravation dissolve in a fit of laughter.

MONDAY

A newcomer at work or in your social circle could raise a few eyebrows, including your own. Don't make premature judgements. You might be in for a surprise.

TUESDAY

Everything points to a period of minor frustrations which you will just have to bear. Don't blow your top.

WEDNESDAY

The values underlying some of your ideals are under attack from several quarters. Are you prepared to admit that extremism is often a failing of yours?

THURSDAY

Use your powers of invention in practical directions. Fantastic flights of fancy will get you labelled an eccentric.

FRIDAY

Hasty words are likely to be the catalyst for a change in a relationship. Will you be the one to utter them?

SATURDAY

Those who are accident prone must make a special effort not to go beyond the safety barrier.

BIRTH NUMBER 9 – DATE NUMBER 7

SUNDAY

Don't allow your enthusiasm to get the better of you. Not everyone will be in the same zestful mood, and if you try to force the issue you could be cold-shouldered in an unexpected quarter.

MONDAY

Pull out all the stops to get what you want where your independent actions are concerned, but too much force too forcefully applied may produce a lack of real cooperation or lasting resentment in others. Persuasion is always better than coercion.

TUESDAY

If you're thinking of entertaining or being entertained, someone with a quick but shallow intelligence may captivate you with new ideas. Don't get carried away. Put to the test, they may contain far more chaff than wheat.

WEDNESDAY

You are strong on vitality at the moment, but weak on logic. A rapid reassessment of the effect of external developments on your own position could put your thoughts in order.

THURSDAY

Love is no respecter of persons. You should remember this if you have set your heart in a particular direction.

FRIDAY

You're apt to hurt others far more than you realise. A lot of offence can be caused by those ill-considered remarks that sometimes jump out of your mouth. You may be too long in the tooth to change completely, but you can limit a lot of the damage if you think before you speak.

SATURDAY

Overdoing it at home as well as at work will make you miserable. Health could be a key issue at the moment.

BIRTH NUMBER 9 – DATE NUMBER 8

SUNDAY

If you're currently feeling low, do you know what is making you miserable? Mistaking the symptoms for the cause is a certain guarantee that there will be little change.

MONDAY

There is a world of difference between versatility and wasting your talents by spreading them too widely and too thinly. Concentrate only on achieving what can be achieved.

TUESDAY

The strength of your wish to be 'somebody' in the eyes of the world fluctuates according to your mood and what distractions are to hand. It is a longing rooted deep in your pysche nevertheless. Ultimately it doesn't matter either way whether you achieve greater status. What is important is that you go on trying to better yourself.

WEDNESDAY

Your connections have served you well in the past, but there are limits to any friendship, even one based on mutual interest. Current problems are best tackled unaided.

THURSDAY

Don't let yourself be lured into a false sense of security where money is concerned. Keep your eyes and ears wide open when threading your way through the financial minefield.

FRIDAY

You may think people are out for what they can get, and recent empty promises will have reinforced your cynicism. But if you are tempted to play the same game, you might forfeit much of your credit with the people who really matter.

SATURDAY

Your thoughts may be going over the events of the last year or so. If the conclusion is that you now need a change of direction somewhere along the line, the right signposts are still some way ahead.

BIRTH NUMBER 9 – DATE NUMBER 9

SUNDAY

Differing interests may cause rifts. You are more likely to react by doing what you want to do, not what you should do, to maintain harmony. If compromise is impossible, then at least practise moderation.

MONDAY

At the moment you are inclined to care too much what others think. But associates and acquaintances care basically only about themselves, so do what you have to do.

TUESDAY

Most people like a gamble now and then. You're no different to anyone else in this respect but, though you hope to win, you must also be prepared to lose.

WEDNESDAY

You could be caught up in a drama. Avoid histrionics yourself and give short shrift to anyone inclined to play to the gallery.

THURSDAY

A kind word or deed may move you, but keep your guard up where the world in general is concerned. One person's generosity of spirit doesn't mean that everyone is full of the milk of human kindness.

FRIDAY

Playing by the rules is not the same thing as toeing the line. No one could cast you in the role of 'Yes man', but rebellion for its own sake is self-defeating.

SATURDAY

If you're inclined to strike a hard bargain emotionally, you should remind yourself that no one's credit is unlimited where their feelings are concerned.

FADIC NUMBERS

Lucky numbers, including fortune indicators for sporting gambles on horses, dogs, football and lotteries, have a part to play in numerology. The numbers are seldom constant – they vary at different times both for people and events (see Chapter 5).

A fadic number, or number of fate, on the other hand, has a regular bearing on a person's life throughout their period on earth. It is a number which exercises an influence at key moments. Its influence is sometimes beneficial, sometimes malignant, in the unfolding of someone's destiny. With the best examples, time and again one number, on occasion two, crops up far more often than it would by coincidence, vitally affecting and perhaps even controlling an individual's fate.

There are many historical examples of this peculiar phenomenon. We have already noted in Chapter 1 the role number 28 played in the life of the great Russian novelist, Leo Tolstoy. Another example is the case of Tolstoy's near contemporary, Count Otto von Bismarck, who was Chancellor of Germany and who personally dominated European politics for much of the latter part of the nineteenth century.

The heraldic crest of his aristocratic Prussian family bore the motto, '*In trinitate fortitudo*' (literally, 'In trinity, strength', or 'Strength in three') – an early sign of the important effect number 3 would have on the significant events in the life and career of a brilliant statesman.

Bismarck served three Hohenzollern monarchs and engineered the creation of the German *Reich* by uniting three political entities: Schleswig-Holstein, the Germanic Confederation and Prussia herself. He consolidated the new Germany's position by defeating France in the third of the three wars he waged. Afterwards his greatest contribution to European stability was the *Dreikaiserbund*, the triple alliance of the Emperors of Germany, Austria and Russia. In Prussia he always faced opposition from three political parties, and on a personal note he owned three estates and had three children.

However, the most famous case of a fadic number dominating the life of an historical figure, and indeed the fate of a whole royal dynasty, is that of the influence of the number 14 on the lives of Henry IV of France and his successors.

His name, Henri de Bourbon, contains 14 letters. He was the 14th King of France who was also King of Navarre. He was born on 14 December 1553 (1 + 5 + 5 + 3 = 14). His first wife, Marguerite de Valois was born on 14 May 1553 (again, 1 + 5 + 5 + 3 = 14). On 14 March 1590 Henry won the greatest battle of his troubled reign at Ivry, but on 14 May of the same year Paris revolted against his rule. On 14 November two years later, the French parliament ratified the papal bull empowering

Pope Gregory XIV to nominate another king to rule after Henry – whom he had excommunicated. Finally on 14 May 1610, the narrowness of the *Rue de la Ferronnerie* through which Henry's carriage was travelling gave an assassin the opportunity he needed to strike the king down as his entourage slowed to negotiate the difficult passageway. By a curious and dramatic irony, 14×4 years earlier, on 14 May 1554, King Henry II had signed a decree ordering the widening of the very same street. However the work was never carried out, an omission which cost Henry IV his life.

The remarkable influence of the fadic 14 on French history does not end there. Henry IV was the founder of the Bourbon dynasty and the monarchs of that line who followed him were also to find the number a potent and frequently harmful influence on their lives.

Henry's son and heir, Louis XIII, was born in 1601 and baptised on 14 September. Fourteen years later, in 1615, he married Anne of Austria. He was to die on 14 May 1643 ($1 + 6 + 4 + 3 = 14$).

Next came the 'Sun King', Louis XIV, obviously the 14th King of France to bear that name. He acceded to the throne in 1643 ($1 + 6 + 4 + 3 = 14$ once more) and died in 1715 ($1 + 7 + 1 + 5 = 14$) at the age of 77 ($7 + 7 = 14$). Born in 1638, 14 is again the result if that year is added to the year of his death ($1638 + 1715 = 3353 = 3 + 3 + 5 + 3 = 14$).

His successor, Louis XV reigned for 59 years ($5 + 9 = 14$). This Louis's reign was comparatively uneventful, but the same cannot be said of the king who followed him on the throne of France. Louis XVI was to lose his head during the excesses of the French Revolution which began on the 14 July with the storming of the *Bastille*, the infamous prison that symbolised the tyranny of the *Ancien Régime*. Fourteen, the number which ushered in the Bourbon dynasty and which had influenced so much of its history, thus proved to be the numerological herald of its downfall.

So much for the fateful power of one number in the lives of the Bourbon kings of France. Moving to contemporary times, another royal figure has a highly proactive fadic number which plays a vital role in her life.

HM Queen Elizabeth II of Britain was born on 21 April 1926. This makes her birth number 7 and she is very typical of the personality type associated with this vibration. However, another number has also had a profound influence for her.

The first indication was provided by the fact that she was born at 2.40 a.m. ($2 + 4 = 6$). Remember that her father was George VI. Remember too that the last number in the year of her birth is also 6. Here are the initial clues that another number might eventually come to determine much of her fate.

The Queen was married on 20 November 1947, so 7 is the final digit in this important year. The whole date reduces to 7 ($20 + 11 + 1 + 9 + 4 + 7 = 52 = 7$). The double 7 reinforces the influence of her birth number on her early life, but as she grew older it is not 7 but 6 which begins to dominate. George VI died on 6 February 1952, so she acceded to the throne on the sixth day of a month, the whole date reducing this time to a repetition of her life number ($6 + 2 + 1 + 9 + 5 + 2 = 25 = 7$). Her coronation took place at Westminster during the sixth month of the following year, making her the sixth woman to become Sovereign of England in her own right.

Her immediate family, once completed, was six in number – herself, Princes Philip, Charles, Andrew, Edward and Princess Anne. All the males have exactly six letters in their names. The last born, Edward, has the birth number 6, which is also the vibration ruling the birth of Queen Elizabeth's sister, Princess Margaret, and incidentally that of her uncle, the fated Duke of Windsor, whose actions indirectly brought her to the throne.

With 6 now so evidently a paramount fadic influence, it should be no surprise that one of the most joyous occasions of Queen Elizabeth's reign was her Silver Jubilee in 1977, the number 77 of course being the double repetition of her birth number and this number reduces to 6 (1 + 9 + 7 + 7 = 24 = 6). Her *annus horribilis*, however, was 1992. In this year she was 66 and witnessed the divorce of her daughter, the breakdown of the marriages of two of her sons, as well as a terrible fire at Windsor Castle. There could be no stronger evidence of the influence of 6 for bad as well as good in Elizabeth II's life.

As for the future, in the year 2002 she will reach the age of 76, so bringing into conjunction the influential life number 7 and the fadic 6. This is likely to be a fateful year both for her and for the House of Windsor over which she has presided for so long.

There is another example of a prominent figure for whom 7 and 6 were major influences. Marilyn Monroe was born Norma Jeane Mortenson on 1 June 1926 which gives her the life number 7, but it is the month and last digit of the year of her birth in combination with 7 that was to prove of enormous fadic significance in her life.

Marilyn married two of her three husbands in June, the sixth month. Her marriage to Joe Di Maggio took place in a different month, but the date reduces to 7 (14 January 1954 = 14 + 1 + 1 + 9 + 5 + 4 = 34 = 7), and throughout her life it is the fadic 6 in conjunction with 7, her birth vibration, that is so striking.

Her last and most famous lover was Robert Kennedy, the US Attorney General and brother of the President, who we now know was very close to her at the end of her life. There are six letters in his first name and seven in his second. For Norma Jeane too, the name she took in her film career has the same numbers, though reversed. Marilyn has seven, Monroe six.

One of Marilyn's most successful films was *The Seven Year Itch*, but the cycle of her own life can be reduced to a simple, rather sad summary; born 1926, died 1962 at age 36. Thus we find 6, the fadic number, reversed with 2 in the years of her birth and of her death. Her age of 36, with its final digit of 6 is the product of multiplying two 6s together. It is possible to speculate about the meaning of the appearance of 2 in this life and death series. Perhaps it reflects the fact that both in reality and in the dualism at the heart of her tragedy there were two people, Norma Jeane and Marilyn – one an ordinary girl from a broken home, the other a screen goddess who ultimately was unable to cope with the pressures of fame. As a postscript to the story, it is worth recalling that her body was taken from her home to the County Morgue in the Los Angeles Department of Justice where it was placed in Crypt 33. As 3 + 3 = 6, it is a chilling reminder of the fact that just as her birth number was 7, her fadic number in life and death was 6.

KEY DATES IN LIFE

Mothers birth date: _____

Father's birth date: _____

Significant dates for parents: _____

_____

_____

Other family dates: _____

_____

_____

Own birth date: _____

Important life events: _____

    Career: _____

_____

    Marriage: _____

    Birth of children: _____

_____

_____

Other important numbers: _____

_____

_____

_____

_____

_____

_____

_____

_____

_____

_____

_____

_____

_____

_____

Unlike the birth number, there is no formula by which a person's fadic number can be worked out in advance. Once established, however, it can have astonishing effects, and may provide real clues about the future. For instance the great pyschic, Count Louis Hamon ('Cheiro') was able to predict the exact day of the death of King Edward VII by observing the early and continuing influence of the numbers 6 and 9 in the monarch's life.

Anyone, not just kings, queens and film stars, can have a fadic number – but this is not always the case. Everyone has a personality vibration determined by birth and this will have a significant influence on their life through the interaction of character with time vibrations, particularly on a day-to-day basis (see Chapter 3). But the birth number is not necessarily the same as the fadic number – a number that has the strange power of intervening decisively in important events or at critical periods. If it is present as a psychic force, it will keep reappearing as a number of destiny as a person's life develops. Through carefully recorded observation you can determine whether you, or someone close to you, has a fadic number with this unique potential.

Use the worksheet opposite to write down the key dates in your life so far, beginning with what you know for certain about your parents' history, so as to determine any fadic force in operation at your birth. Widen the circle to include your own name and the names of your family. Add in important dates not only in your family life but in your business career too. Check to see whether significant events occur at regular intervals which can be expressed by number. In fact list everything of importance that has touched you so far in life by way of number.

This process could well reveal that one number, perhaps two, does have a profound effect on your earthly journey.

If this turns out to be the case, the fadic number will almost certainly remain active for the rest of your days, and you will be able to recognise the phenomenon each time it occurs. Whether you will be able to take measures to counter its influence, however, is open to question, even if that is your wish. Using your own free will may change the course of events for you, but whether your progress in life at vital points is decided by chance, coincidence, or the unconscious or conscious exercise of forces within you, that progress will always be your destiny, and you cannot escape it.

WINNING NUMBERS

Chapter 4 shows that fadic numbers are very far from being lucky numbers. As numbers of destiny, their influence can be bad as well as good. Nor is it usual for an individual to have a fortunate number which confers benefit throughout life. Rather, lucky numbers change according to circumstance.

Such vibrations can often be identified, and for this reason numerology may be a powerful ally in various forms of betting. So whether it is horses or greyhounds – which carry a number in races for identification purposes – or football matches – which are assigned a number on pools coupons – or a national lottery, numbers can be linked to all the most popular gambles.

The justification for using numerology as an aid to successful betting lies in the fact that some numbers are definitely favoured in particular conjunctions, depending on the gamble being pursued. But they are not infallible so, for speculative wagers which depend on chance, no one should stake more than they can reasonably afford to lose on any of the indications given below. Even without certainty or absolute guarantees of success, when the numerological vibrations point in a certain direction, you may be able to take advantage of their forecast of what is likely to happen.

HORSES

The following numerological method may bring a fair level of success in the risky business of backing horses. It is based on the fact that different numbers are best in different types of race and over different race distances. The key to it is this table:

Flat

Non-handicaps	1 and 2
Handicaps	
5 furlongs	1 and 2
6 furlongs	2 and 3
7 furlongs or a mile	4 and 5
9–12 furlongs	6 and 7
13 furlongs or more	8 and 9

National Hunt

Non-handicaps	1 and 2

Handicaps

Under 3 miles	1 and 2
3 miles or more	3 and 4

Note that a distinction is drawn between races which are handicaps and those which are not. If you are not familiar with the mysteries of backing horses, you can tell if a race is a handicap or not by looking at the race-card or the card in your morning newspaper. Any race not clearly labelled a 'handicap' is automatically a conditions or non-handicap race.

In handicaps, the favoured numbers depend on the distance of the race. Race distances are stated on race cards and in all morning papers. Flat racing is broken down into five categories of distance. Jumpers, however, are much less specialists in this regard, and under National Hunt rules, it is sufficient to differentiate between races of less than 3 miles and those over 3 miles.

This is a numerological approach, but there are sound, additional 'form' reasons why 1 and 2 are the favoured numbers in non-handicaps, whereas an adjacent pair of numbers from 1 to 9 are best for handicaps depending on their distance.

Note that the above table is only a guide to probable results, and a choice is offered between the two favoured numbers in each pair for any given race. When the odds on offer are high enough, it may be possible to bet on both numbers and to show a good gain whichever wins.

To make this absolutely clear, and also to provide some idea of what numerology can achieve in backing horses, here are full details for Wednesday afternoon's racing at June 1993 Royal Ascot meeting – a fixture which always features some of the most competititve sport of the entire Flat season. Betting odds appear after placed horses.

Royal Ascot   Wednesday, 16 June 1993

2.30 pm	*Jersey Stakes* (Non-handicap)	
	No. 1 Ardkinglass Won 10/1	
	No. 2 Eurolink Thunder	
3.05 pm	*Queen Mary Stakes* (Non-handicap)	
	No. 1 Double Down	
	No. 2 Elrafa Ah 3rd 14/1	
3.45 pm	*Coronation Stakes* (Non-handicap)	
	No. 1 Elizabeth Bay 2nd 7/2	
	No. 2 Gold Splash Won 100/30	
4.20 pm	*Royal Hunt Cup* (Handicap; 1 mile)	
	No. 4 Tapis Rouge	
	No. 5 Imperial Ballet Won 20/1	
4.55 pm	*Queen's Vase* (Non-handicap)	
	No. 1 Acanthus	
	No. 2 Blue Grotto	
5.30 pm	*Bessborough Stakes* (Handicap; 1m 4f)	
	No. 6 Last Embrace 4th 10/1	
	No. 7 Fieldridge Non-runner	

Three winners (at 10/1, 100/30 and 20/1) made it quite a day for numerologists! Of course winners like these cannot be expected every time, but this set of results, and many others any racing day, would certainly make the racing experts sit up and take notice. No guarantees, but when the numerical vibrations are working strongly, a lot of winners may be the result.

GREYHOUNDS

Numerology can be a great help to the greyhound enthusiast. Six dogs per race at most tracks mean that it is only necessary to make correct assumptions about the numbers 1 to 6 some of the time to give a reasonable chance of an overall gain. As with horses, nothing is certain, but anyone using the following method should find a share of the winners. There may be good meetings, and some much less so, but on balance there is no reason why the study of numbers should not do just as well as more conventional ways of choosing which dogs to back.

Nowadays most greyhound meetings feature 12 races in an afternoon or evening. There is plenty of time, therefore, to find out from early races which numbers are especially favoured on a given occasion. So the idea is to wait until the first four races have been run before risking a bet.

In each of these races note down which number was the winner and which was placed second. The number to bet on to win in the remainder of the races at the meeting is the one which has recorded the most wins and places after the fourth race has been run. In the event of a tie between two or more numbers, take the highest.

Also, find the number which achieved the second greatest total of wins and seconds in the first four races. This gives a second number to bet on in reversed forecasts with the number to be backed for a win. In the event of a tie, this time take the lowest number. Bets on reversed forecasts by which two numbers are backed to finish first and second in either order invariably pay much better odds than straightforward bets for a win.

It would be wrong, however, to expect too much from this or any other way of choosing which dogs to bet on. No one number can win all the races, or anything like it, any more than one person is consistently able to pick out the majority of the winners. So if you are fortunate enough to find three winners, you should have no more bets to win for the rest of the meeting. Similarly one winning forecast will usually be good enough to show a profit on balance, and it is unreasonable to expect multiple successes from a bet which is quite difficult to land. So, after one win from forecast bets, pocket your winnings and cease betting on the two-number combinations in whatever races are left to be run.

Examples are given below of the main greyhound meetings featured nationally by the big bookmakers. These were run on the same afternoon as the Royal Ascot meeting used as an example for horse racing. To give a full illustration of the working of the method, however, the afternoon cards from the Tuesday and Thursday of that week have also been included.

Hackney
Tuesday, 15 June 1993

1.48 pm   4–6
2.05 pm   6–5
2.26 pm   3–1
2.42 pm   1–6

Trap to bet on to win is 6 with 1 in reversed forecasts

3.03 pm   3–2
3.20 pm   6–3   3/1 winner
3.37 pm   3–2
3.55 pm   6–1   5/1 winner, £19.78 winning forecast,
                no more forecast bets
4.18 pm   6–2   2/1 winner, no more win bets
4.37 pm   3–5
4.54 pm   4–2
5.11 pm   3–6

Ramsgate
Tuesday, 15 June 1993

1.55 pm   5–2
2.12 pm   3–1
2.33 pm   4–2
2.50 pm   5–4

Trap to bet on to win is 5 with 2 in reversed forecasts

3.11 pm   2–5   £10.70 winning forecast,
                no more forecast bets
3.28 pm   5–3   7/2 winner
3.43 pm   1–4
4.04 pm   2–6
4.24 pm   2–4
4.43 pm   1–4
5.04 pm   3–2
5.19 pm   4–1

Hove
Wednesday, 16 June 1993

1.47 pm   4–6
2.07 pm   1–3
2.27 pm   6–4
2.47 pm   5–6

Trap to bet on to win is 6 with 4 in reversed forecasts

3.07 pm   6–4   2/1 winner, £9.82 winning forecast,
                no more forecast bets
3.27 pm   6–1   5/4 winner
3.47 pm   5–4
4.07 pm   1–3
4.27 pm   1–5
4.47 pm   4–1
5.07 pm   4–3
5.27 pm   6–4   5/4 winner

Crayford
Thursday, 17 June 1993

1.48 pm   2–4
2.05 pm   4–2
2.26 pm   2–1
2.42 pm   4–6

Trap to bet on to win is 4 with 2 in reversed forecasts

3.03 pm   3–6
3.20 pm   6–1
3.37 pm   3–4
3.55 pm   4–2   9/2 winner, £23.50 winning forecast,
                no more forecast bets
4.18 pm   4–2   11/4 winner
4.37 pm   5–2
4.54 pm   2–6
5.11 pm   4–2   9/4 winner

Using basic unit stakes of, say, £1 for a win bet and £2 on each of the reversed forecasts, there was an overall gain at all four meetings. Thus with greyhounds, as with horses, even if you know little about the sport and have a bet only occasionally, you may win with the help of numerology.

FOOTBALL POOLS

The Treble Chance featured on football coupons is a huge gamble, and it is doubtful whether numerology can assist readers to make a big win probable, any more than any other method that can be devised. The odds against success are so great that only extreme good fortune will bring success and an enormous payout.

However the proper use of numerical power can be of some help in cutting this formidable challenge down to size. Below are the numbers

on the pools coupon arranged in a rectangle in which each separate vertical column contains all the numbers with the same final digit.

1	2	3	4	5	6	7	8	9	10
11	12	13	14	15	16	17	18	19	20
21	22	23	24	25	26	27	28	29	30
31	32	33	34	35	36	37	38	39	40
41	42	43	44	45	46	47	48	49	50
51	52	53	54	55	56	57	58		

What happens on the pools most weeks is that the draws are not clus-
tered in only a few of the vertical columns in this rectangle. Rather, they
are spaced out evenly across it, with just one or two of them in each
downward column. You can check this for yourself by looking at a few
recent entries you have made.

This can be taken into account as follows. Write down on a piece of
paper the 58 match numbers on the coupon in 10 vertical rows to form
the above rectangle. Now circle one number in each row, taking care that
you choose from a wide range of horizontal rows, so as to get the kind of
distribution which usually wins. You can help your winning chances
even more by circling a roughly equal total of odd and even numbers.

This will give 10 matches to be transferred to your coupon for the
well-known full cover type of entry favoured by many pools investors.
The instructions written alongside the 10 crosses are: 'Perm any eight
from 10 = 45 lines', followed by the stake per line and the total cost of the
permutation, depending on which coupon you enter.

If you wish to stake on 11 selections, a full cover perm of 165 lines
is involved, whereas 12 selections require 495 lines. For 11 selections you
would be able to have an extra number from any vertical row of your
choice, with one number from each of the other nine rows. With 12
crosses, you would have an additional number in each of two columns
or, if you prefer, three numbers from one column with one each in the
remainder.

If you had the great good luck to win the Treble Chance using this
idea, you would have an unequivocal demonstration of the power that
numbers can exercise in your life.

NATIONAL LOTTERY

Finally, the mysterious power of numbers can be harnessed to assist you
in finding your numbers for a lottery. In a national lottery such as in the
UK, with such gigantic odds against winning a really big prize, there are
no guarantees of success – but in a game of pure chance, lucky numbers
have as good a chance as any other system of selection.

Below is the ancient magical Square of Venus which includes every
number from 1 to 49, just like the balls in the UK Lottery. The square is
so arranged that each of its 16 lines – seven horizontal, seven vertical and
two diagonal – adds up to a total of 175. Because of this strange property
it has been used for centuries by mystics and soothsayers for various
occult purposes. Today it is ideal for the divination of Lottery numbers.

22	47	16	41	10	35	4
5	23	48	17	42	11	29
30	6	24	49	18	36	12
13	31	7	25	43	19	37
38	14	32	1	26	44	20
21	39	8	33	2	27	45
46	15	40	9	34	3	28

To make your own personal Lottery forecast, find your birth number in the magic square. If the date number of the day on which the Lottery draw is to take place is an even number, the numbers in the horizontal line containing your birth number should be used in your forecast. If the date number of the draw is an odd number, however, you should use the vertical line. The method of calculating the date number is explained on page 93.

In this way you can find five numbers to enter each week in addition to your birth number. If you are making an entry of several lines, the numbers in both the horizontal and vertical lines of the square controlled by your personal number will be your inspiration, and you will have the legendary luck of Venus on your side!

Few of us will be fortunate enough to win an enourmous sum of course, but in all gambling games, as in life itself, luck, chance, fate – call it what you will – may be harnessed and sometimes even regulated to make the best of things as they are and will be. The 'winning numbers' explained in this chapter could be lucky for you.

. . . IN CONCLUSION

The core of Pythagoras's philosophy may be summarised as a theory of number, in part rationalistic, in part mystic, which seeks to provide an explanation of the *kosmos* and to relate this to the deepest workings of the human soul. Here *kosmos*, anglicised to 'cosmos', did not have its later meaning of 'the universe'. In the original Greek it simply meant 'ornament' and in the Pythagorean sense 'the beautiful order of things'. His teachings were eventually recorded and became available to scholars from the fourth century BC onwards. Since then numerology has undergone a continuous process of development, with later writers and mystics focusing on the humanistic aspects of Pythagoras's speculations about the soul. By an empirical method of observation and experiment, they began to build up personality profiles which can be attached to each of the primary numbers of birth, 1 to 9, and in special cases to the master numbers11 and 22. Chapter 2 of this book is the most complete, modern statement available anywhere of the wisdom of the ages in this respect.

Anyone who reads the relevant profiles cannot fail to be impressed by their descriptive accuracy. Applied intelligently they can help you to know yourself better, thereby enabling you to make the most of the positive elements of your character, as well as minimising your more negative characteristics and diverting them into positive channels. In your dealings with other people, an understanding of what really makes them tick will assist you in communicating with them better leading to a more rewarding relationship not only in your private and social life, but in the world of work and business, too.

The Lifeguide enlarges Pythagoras's ideas on numerical vibration relative to the rhythm of time. Consulting the Lifeguide will give you the opportunity to examine your problems less subjectively and with a more open mind. By understanding number and its power in your life, you will acquire a fuller, more rounded perspective on the unravelling of your destiny. You will then be able to fit events into a unified pattern of development unique to yourself, and so enhance your understanding of your place in the world as well as that of others, and even of the world itself.

Modern numerology can therefore have great value, and this book shows you how to harness and use that worth. Constant reference to all sections of it may help you to feel less at the mercy of an uncertain fate and more in control of your journey through life as the pages of time unfurl. If this turns out to be the case, *The Numerology Handbook* will have served its purpose.